Crash Course in Marketing for Libraries

Recent Titles in
Crash Course Series

Crash Course in Marketing for Libraries

Second Edition

Susan W. Alman and Sara Gillespie Swanson

Crash Course

AN IMPRINT OF ABC-CLIO, LLC
Santa Barbara, California • Denver, Colorado • Oxford, England

Library of Congress Cataloging-in-Publication Data

Alman, Susan Webreck.
   Crash course in marketing for libraries / Susan W. Alman and
Sara Gillespie Swanson. — Second edition.
      pages cm. — (Crash course)

   Includes bibliographical references and index.
   ISBN 978-1-61069-870-2 (pbk : alk. paper) —
ISBN 978-1-61069-871-9 (ebook)   1. Libraries—Marketing.
2. Libraries—Public relations.   I. Swanson, Sara Gillespie.   II. Title.

   Z716.3.A46   2015
   021.7—dc23   2014026782

ISBN: 978-1-61069-870-2
EISBN: 978-1-61069-871-9

19   18   17   16   15   1   2   3   4   5

This book is also available on the World Wide Web as an eBook.
Visit www.abc-clio.com for details.

Libraries Unlimited
An Imprint of ABC-CLIO, LLC

ABC-CLIO, LLC
130 Cremona Drive, P.O. Box 1911
Santa Barbara, California 93116-1911

This book is printed on acid-free paper ∞

Manufactured in the United States of America

Copyright Acknowledgments

The author and publisher gratefully acknowledge permission to reprint the following materials found in the appendices of this book:

Abington Community Library, "Just Jeans in January" flyer (Appendix F); Newsletter, "From the Stacks" Winter 2013 (Appendix I); Sample press release (Appendix K).

Avon Grove Library, Avon Grove Library Annual Appeal, 2013 (Appendix G); 2013 Librarian's Annual Report (Appendix H).

Cedar Rapids Public Library, Cedar Rapids, IA, and *Lawrence Public Library,* Lawrence, KS, John Cotton Dana Award Application (Appendix D)

Mid-Continent Public Library, Independence, MO, Brand Communication Plan (Appendix E)

Mt. Lebanon Public Library, Pittsburgh, PA, Newsletters: Friend's Group, December 2013, January 2014, February 2014, March 2014 (Appendix I); Information Guide (Appendix F): Chair-ity Flyer (Appendix J). Reprinted with permission from Cynthia K. Richey, Director, Mt. Lebanon Public Library, Pittsburgh, PA.

Benicia Public Library, Benicia, CA, 2012–2013 Annual Report (Appendix H)

Grand Rapids Public Library, Grand Rapids, MI, 2013 Annual Report (Appendix H). Photos reprinted with permission from Terry Johnston Photography/www.terryjohnstonphoto.com

McMinnville Public Library, McMinnville, MO, March–May 2014 McMinnville Friends of the Library Newsletter (Appendix J).

Contents

Introduction

We, librarians, know that libraries provide value to our communities and to society, and for the most part our users recognize the benefits that they receive. Nonusers of libraries rarely argue against the value of libraries, but they often do not recognize or are not aware of the many services that librarians and libraries provide. They need to be made aware, especially in an era of increasing budget cuts, but this task is not solely the responsibility of the library's director.

To the uninitiated, anyone who works in a library is perceived as a "librarian" whether he or she is a custodian, volunteer, or director. Your entire library staff should be coached on how to be library advocates and how to market the library to everyone they meet. This guide will help you train your staff to do just that. It offers basic information on how to market libraries to people who work in a library, anyone who uses a library, and perhaps most importantly, the nonuser of a library's services.

This edition of *Crash Course in Marketing for Librarians* includes lessons learned from library marketing experiences over the past two decades and also information about ways to use social media to inform your community about library resources and services. The information and examples provided will equip you with the skills you need to develop a plan to communicate with the community served by your library.

Each marketing and public relations plan is unique since marketing activities are based on the needs of the library's community or the areas of interest and expertise of the librarians; however, there are basic skills and processes that should be applied in each setting. This practical approach to marketing will provide you with examples of marketing ideas, plans, and projects that have been successfully implemented in libraries. Small projects have developed into major transformations and those involved have become change agents for all types of libraries in which they have worked or volunteered. Here are some examples of projects and positions that have been undertaken by librarians and students who have used the marketing and public relations skills covered in this publication:

- Student-led class project to:
  - Develop, distribute, and analyze the data from a community questionnaire to determine the need and potential use of a library outpost
  - Develop the new collection
  - Design the layout of the library, order the furnishings, and install the materials
  - Create the marketing plan and public relations materials
  - Plan the opening gala
  - Assess the project and publish the results
- Creation of award-winning marketing plans and continued leadership in library marketing and public relations
  - Writing of marketing publications
  - Library positions focused on marketing in all types of settings
- Marketing consultants and marketing workshop presenters

This book has been developed from the content and activities used in our experiences as librarians, library marketing course instructors, and from the technologies that are being used to connect with users and nonusers. The success of your marketing efforts can be realized if you follow these *Crash Course* guidelines. You are sure to have fun as well as make a difference in your library and the community it serves.

Chapter 1

The Planning Process for Your Marketing Plan

The development of a planning document is the basis for effective organizational management and the planning process is one that managers should embrace rather than avoid. A solid strategic plan takes time and resources to create, but the manager can use the goals and objectives to plan for programs and services, collection development, budget justification, and marketing and public relations. In this chapter, we will show you how to create a basic strategic plan that will serve as the foundation for you to then develop an effective marketing and public relations plan.

Since the ultimate goal is to develop a marketing campaign, it is important to develop a strategic plan that is focused on fulfilling the mission of the library. You will learn how to collect information about your community and then about ways to analyze your community's needs. Finally, we take a look at the best marketing method(s) to use based on your library's resources.

Remember that just a little knowledge can go a long way in giving you the skills necessary to begin a marketing campaign in your library. But the most important thing you need for marketing is enthusiasm! Many procedures can be followed to develop an effective marketing campaign, but your time and effort will be wasted if your coworkers and volunteers are uninterested. First, you need to engage your staff and volunteers and get them involved in the library's activities, and then you can address your community.

Defining Marketing

Before you can begin to market your library, you have to know what marketing means to you. At the beginning of class, we ask students to provide their definitions of marketing and from the responses it is clear that marketing has different connotations. Marketing components include:

- A process to meet the organization's mission
- Educating the users about programs and services
- Deciding which programs and services benefit the target audience
- Understanding the community in order to promote programs and services
- Advertising or outreach

Library marketing involves understanding the interests of your community, identifying the services that they want or need, creating the services that will appeal to the users, and then effectively educating the users about those services. Gathering this information is not serendipitous. As noted in the next section, there is a specific process to follow when developing the marketing plan.

The Marketing Planning Process

The plan that you will develop to market your library's services should match the goals and objectives of your library's strategic plan. If your library already has a strategic plan, you should use it to guide your vision of what programs and services you want to develop and how you'll market them to the community. For instance, if one of the goals and objectives of your library's strategic plan is to reach preschool children and their caregivers, your marketing plan should target this audience. That way, your marketing plan will fit in with your strategic plan. Below are examples of how the strategic goal and marketing goal fit together.

Library A: Comparison of Strategic Plan Goal and Marketing Plan Goal

- Strategic Plan Goal—Act as an agent of innovation for the community
- Marketing Plan Goal—Create a maker space for the community

Library B: Comparison of Strategic Plan Goal and Marketing Plan Goal

- Strategic Plan Goal—Enhance library usage through partnerships, programs, and promotions
- Marketing Plan Goal—Develop partnerships with local school, community centers, and businesses

---

What should you do if your library doesn't have a strategic plan? Many libraries are not guided by a strategic plan, but this shouldn't preclude the development of a marketing plan. If your library doesn't have a strategic plan, the first steps in planning your marketing campaign include the following process to create a clear vision:

- Determine what the target audience needs (community analysis)
- Determine the ways in which the library can fulfill the needs of the target audience

The results of this process can be articulated in the form of goals and objectives that will be used to guide the project. A "goal" is a statement about what you want to accomplish, and an "objective" is a statement that identifies how you are going to achieve that goal. If you clearly state your goals and objectives, everyone in your library will know exactly what to work toward. The examples below show how objectives are the specific ways to reach the broader goals.

Goals	Objective 1	Objective 2
Enhance library usage through partnerships, programs, and promotions	Encourage nonusers to get and use a library card	Reach out to students and families
Promote lifelong learning	Provide resources that target key segments of the population, children, teens, senior citizens, immigrants	Partner with education and business to provide a diverse mix of programs to the target groups

Goals, objectives, and the marketing plan cannot be developed until you have a solid understanding of your community. Often librarians have a great marketing idea, and they expend a lot of time and energy developing it without ever considering whether the project or program is relevant to their community. It isn't until the anticipated result hasn't been realized (attendance was poor or circulation was not increased) that people recognize the importance of consulting the intended audience prior to planning. It's easy to get caught up in the excitement of an idea and forget this first step, even though it seems obvious that determining what the community wants is critical. There are countless examples of how librarians have miscalculated the needs of their users or how they have not anticipated all of the factors that could have dire effects on the program or service. Here are two cases of people who had good intentions for the library, but didn't employ basic planning techniques.

Case 1: A well-meaning librarian with an avid interest in Madame Curie planned an elaborate celebration of the scientist's birthday with activities and refreshments for the anticipated teen participants. Sadly, the librarian never consulted with the potential audience or relevant teachers at the local school to determine if the students were studying Madame Curie in science or history classes, if the students were interested in Madame Curie, or if there were other important events scheduled on the day of the library program. In addition, the only information about this event was posted on the library's website. As a result the time, energy, and money spent on this library event was wasted because not a single person attended. While it would have taken extra time initially to get input from students and teachers about the interest and viability of a birthday party for Madame Curie, the library could have avoided an expensive mistake. Asking this target group about their ideas for a library program (community analysis) would have had a better chance of attracting an audience than an unvetted idea.

Case 2: A library without the benefit of a strategic plan and a library board of directors handpicked by the board president embarked on a costly venture without conducting a community analysis. The summer-reading program was the largest project undertaken by this library and the participation rate of 1,000 had decreased by more than 10 percent in a two-year period. Rather than conducting a community survey to determine why the program had decreased or to ask for alternative ideas, the president of the library board, a former scientist, took it upon himself to write a $5 million grant to establish a STEM (Science, Technology, Engineering, and Mathematics)-based summer reading program. Undaunted when the grant was not funded, the board president made arrangements for STEM-literacy training for the library staff and then secured a passing vote from the library board members to pay $4,000 for four days of training. While fiscal responsibility must be a concern, the most important point is to gather information from the community before implementing a new product or service. Having another year of decreased attendance in the summer-reading program coupled with an exorbitant expense could have been avoided if the community had an opportunity to provide input about programs and services.

Gathering Data about Your Community

The first step in determining how to promote your library to the community is to gather information about that community. This section reviews methods that can be used to collect this information: census data, surveys, observation, focus groups, and the nominal group technique (NGT).

Census Data

United States census data is available in a variety of useful formats from various sources. Here are a couple of ideas for how to find census data about your community:

- A comparison of public libraries based on factors such as geographic location, size of collection, staff, or budget, or per capita allocation can be used in preparing a strategic or marketing plan. One online source that is readily available is: https://harvester.census.gov/imls/compare/.

- The *American Fact Finder* based on U.S. census data provides information about a community's demographics: age, education, sex, race, and income. This type of demographic data enables the librarian to compare demographics within each zip code and to note the changes between surveys conducted in different years. This type of overview is helpful in understanding the current community; see http://factfinder2 .census.gov/faces/nav/jsf/pages/index.html.

Surveys

Surveys can be a very valuable means of gathering information about your community's needs, but it's important that you determine exactly what information you want before you write and then conduct a survey. Survey construction is critical to the effective collection of relevant information, so take the time to create questions that will give you the answers you need. Remember that people are very busy, and trying to get them to complete a survey is a challenge. You want to have a survey that is clear and concise and collects the exact information desired. Recently, we received a survey that asked about our individual preferences for continuing education coursework but didn't ask for our preferences on how the courses should be delivered (in-person/online or synchronous/asynchronous), the length of courses, the cost of courses, or graduate credit/noncredit. The survey probably would have been much more useful to its authors if it had asked about these preferences.

The first step in creating an effective survey is to make a list of all the kinds of information you need. Writing the questions takes practice, so test out your survey on some library users, staff, or neighbors before sending it out. Following are some additional hints on constructing a survey:

- Determine whether another librarian has used a survey to gather information about a similar topic and ask if you can borrow it. Also review the literature. Many articles may be in the "how we did it well" category, but the authors are often willing to share everything about their study. If you called and said, "Do you mind if I use your survey? Do you mind if I use this idea?" many librarians would give you all kinds of helpful hints.

- Make the survey as clear and concise as possible. People will be more inclined to answer a survey if it takes five minutes or less.

- Surveys should include questions that will elicit the types of responses that are needed.

- Questions should be
  - relevant to the topic,
  - forced choice (providing lots of options),
  - clearly stated,
  - unbiased,
  - written at a sixth-grade reading level, and
  - focused on one topic (not combining two questions into one).

- Reward the people who respond (with a coupon to a local store, waiver of a book fine, a candy bar, etc.).

Once you have chosen the questions you wish to have answered, decide what kind of survey you will conduct—oral or print. If you would like to do an oral survey, you must decide whether to call potential respondents or survey them in person. If you think that it will be better for you to do a print survey, you must decide whether you want to mail the survey, present it in person, or offer it online—either to a targeted or untargeted audience.

Each of these methods has its benefits and drawbacks. For instance, online surveys can be distributed quickly, and you will save the costs of printing and mailing the survey. Free survey tools like Survey Monkey make online surveys easier than ever. In a print survey, however, the average rate of return is less than 70 percent and often lower than 40 percent. This means you might not be getting a representative cross-section of the population.

Table 1.1 shows the advantages and disadvantages of each method.

Table 1.1. Advantages and Disadvantages of Survey Methods

	ORAL		TARGETED PRINT			UNTARGETED
	Phone	*In-person*	*Mail*	*In-person*	*Online*	*Online*
Advantages	Immediate response	Immediate response		Immediate response	Immediate response	Information gathered from a potential wide range of users and nonusers
	Respondents can be selected		Respondents can be selected		Respondents can be selected	
			Potential to reach a wide range of respondents		Potential to reach a wide range of respondents	
					Ability to quickly analyze responses	
Disadvantages	$–$$$ Telemarketing charges—Volunteers or paid staff	$–$$$ Telemarketing charges—Volunteers or paid staff	$$$ Printing and mailing		E-mail addresses change often	Data from respondents who may be outside of community.
		Respondents are random	Delayed response	Respondents are random	Delayed response	
		High rate of return	Low rate of return	High rate of return		
Considerations	Time consuming Potential annoyance	Time consuming Potential annoyance	Respondent must have ability to read	Respondent must have ability to read	Respondent must have ability to read	

There are additional considerations:

- Paper surveys have to be printed and require either oral or written responses. The data need to be tallied either manually or entered into an electronic system.
- Mailed surveys must include return postage to increase the rate of return.
- Distributing paper surveys in the library will probably result in a higher rate of return, but you only get people who already use the library.
- In order to obtain responses from nonusers, you must identify the audience and how you will reach them.
- Not everyone has access to the Internet to complete an online survey.

Print Survey Distribution

- Inside the library or outside the entrance
- Community gatherings
  - Public events: school plays, athletic games, community days
  - Community centers, businesses, churches

Online Survey Distribution

- E-mail blast to library users
- Paying for a list prepared by an outside entity
- Posting a link to the survey using social media or public websites

Observation

If you want to know whether something is being used in your library, just look around. One of our favorite unobtrusive measures of observation was a library exhibit with a glass case. At the end of every day the librarians would note how many fingerprints or nose prints were on the case to see if people had been engaged with the exhibit. If no fingerprints were observed, the librarians knew that this exhibit did not appeal to the library's users. They could then rethink what kind of exhibits would attract both users and nonusers to the library.

Of course, there are many different ways to do this kind of observation in your library. For instance, before you re-shelve items, conduct counts to see what kind of materials patrons are looking at. If books on one topic or of one genre seem popular, you may want to add more of these books to your collection. Take time to think about what you can observe in your library that will provide clues about the programs and services your patrons desire.

Collecting online usage data is also another type of observation. Usage records will provide information on the unique number of visitors to the website, pages, and catalog, the types of searches that were made, and number of transactions. Plotting these data in visualization charts provides an opportunity to observe the virtual library traffic. If patrons visit particular pages of your website often, you may want to highlight this information on your homepage.

Focus Groups

Focus groups are a useful way to collect information, but they are more costly than surveys and observation because of the time needed to select and interview the groups, record the data, and analyze the information. It is important that you take the time to preselect the audience and gather a group that is representative of the population you have targeted in your strategic or marketing plan. For instance, if your marketing focus is on teens, you should gather a group of teens that represent a cross-section of the entire community. The library staff should know the characteristics of the community and be able to identify key people who should be part of your focus group. Once you know whom you'd like to have in your focus group, prepare a special invitation to get the participants to the meeting. It's important for people to feel that you especially want their opinions on the topic in order to generate their desire to participate.

Many large urban libraries conduct focus groups to enhance their planning. Focus group sessions are arranged in various locations and neighborhoods and during various days and times during the week in order to enable the users and potential users to have a voice in the library's programs and services: mothers, professional workers, business members and business owners, and a variety of people from teens through seniors can be part of the targeted groups. It is important to retain the same facilitator for each session in order to control bias and to ensure that the same questions are used.

Additional costs may be associated with focus groups beyond the staff time it takes to conduct them. For instance, most focus group discussions are recorded and transcribed, so you will need to consider transcription costs for the focus groups you conduct. Also, you may need to provide refreshments during the group meetings. Be sure to factor in all these costs when deciding whether to use a focus group to gather information about your community.

Nominal Group Technique

Nominal group technique (NGT) is a nonthreatening method used to collect responses from each person in a group setting. There are variations in how this process is used, and explanations of setting up a NGT session are readily available on the Internet. The goal of NGT is to provide a setting for each individual to contribute his or her ideas one at a time and to have a group discussion after all the ideas have been generated. We like to use NGT because it is a way for everyone to participate in a nonthreatening environment. Each idea is considered for its merit, and each individual in the group votes anonymously for the top choices. The final vote cannot be contested because the ballots are available for everyone to see.

NGT can be used in groups of about 10 to 12 people to generate ideas for a long-range plan or a short-term project. Before the session begins, the facilitator distributes the objective of the discussion and asks the participants to prepare a list of ideas. At the beginning of the session the facilitator allows additional time for each person in the group to write his or her ideas on paper before sharing them with the group.

The facilitator writes each individual's idea on a board or on a flipchart so that everyone in the group can see it. Each person shares one idea per round, and the facilitator continues the rounds until all the ideas have been generated. Ideas are explained by someone who was not the originator of the suggestion, thus providing an environment to protect "shy" contributors from the need to defend their contribution and "boisterous" contributors will not get the floor to promote their ideas.

Each individual selects the five suggestions that he or she likes best and writes them on either an index card or a Post-It™ note. The individual ranks the five suggestions and places the ranked order on the card, 5 being the highest score and 1 being the lowest. Either the anonymous Post-It™ ballots are "stuck" beside the corresponding idea on the flipchart or board, or the index cards are collected and tallied. Those suggestions that received the highest scores are then debated by the group and prioritized.

For more information on using NGT, see Appendix C.

Analyzing Your Community's Needs

Now that you have gathered information about your community, it's critical that you develop a structured way to consider all the different circumstances or situations that will have an effect on your library. Working in a vacuum without knowledge of what is important to your community can be an expensive mistake if the library program or service is never used. A variety of assessment methods are available to determine the external and internal factors that can affect the use of your library. This chapter discusses two of the most helpful: the environmental scan and SWOT (strengths, weaknesses, opportunities, threats) analysis.

Environmental Scan

A number of interchangeable terms are used to define the process of examining the various factors that may have an impact on the library and the community. You may be familiar with terms such as *community analysis, needs assessment*, and *user analysis*; we prefer to use the term *environmental scan*, because it is a more accurate description of the data collection analysis that provides the information you need to make strategic decisions.

An environmental scan is done for each library to determine what factors and issues are affecting that library or the marketing project. You don't want to work without pertinent information, so you will look at all the different circumstances that will have an impact on your library. By doing so, you can get information about your location, your target market, and your community.

For instance, if your target market is preschool children and their caregivers, what kinds of things do you think will affect this population? What would make them want to use the library or not want to use the library? To answer these questions, you should use a combination of the data collection methods listed in the previous section: surveys, observation, and focus groups. You could also look at census data to give you a clear picture of who is in your community and what trends you may be able to expect. By engaging in an environmental analysis, you can get a very clear picture of your target market and the things your library needs to do to attract this market.

To see an example of a massive environmental scan, take a look at OCLC's *Perceptions of Libraries, 2010*. This environmental scan is an update to OCLC's 2005 scan called *Perceptions of Libraries and Information Resources: A Report to the OCLC Membership*. Although it's unlikely that you'll ever do an environmental scan on this level, it will give you a good idea of the kind of information you can collect by performing one. Because OCLC gathered data about many types of libraries, you also may be able to use data from these studies to extract information that pertains to your situation.

SWOT Analysis

As organizations prepare to develop strategic plans, they often engage in a SWOT (strengths, weaknesses, opportunities, threats) analysis, which is simply a tool that can be used to assess the internal and external factors affecting the environment. These analyses can be elaborate studies that examine a range of activities, from an analysis of the gross revenue of regional businesses to the preferences of a certain segment of the population, or they may be general overviews of the community and the organization. As you can imagine, this type of analysis also can be used to develop your library's marketing plan.

How do you assess each of the SWOT factors? A SWOT analysis may be conducted by means of

- an informal brainstorming session of staff members,
- focus groups,
- formal study by an appointed task force or committee,
- surveys,
- census data,
- talking to users, or
- reading the local newspaper.

Let's begin by addressing each component individually.

When considering library *strengths*, make sure you consider both external and internal ones, which might include the following:

- Internal:
    - Knowledgeable, friendly staff
    - Ample technology to support personal computer usage, 3D printing, or gaming
    - One of best collections in specific area
    - Location in relation to community served:
        - In heart of community
        - Lots of free parking
        - Close to other governmental agencies
- External:
    - Other reasons for people to come to that area:
        - Restaurants, shops, other sites that potential users visit
    - Library is considered the third space.

Next you need to identify the *weaknesses* of the library, staff, and community. Following are some examples of potential internal and external weaknesses:

- Internal:
    - Collection not up-to-date due to budget cuts
    - Technology is out-of-date
    - Understaffed
    - Staff morale has a negative effect on users
- External:
    - Library is off beaten path and difficult to get to by public transportation
    - Parking not available
    - Hours not convenient
    - Community population decreasing
    - Competition increasing:
        - Potential users spend time in other venues
        - Difficult to recruit staff or volunteers to area or institution

It is important to recognize that not all strengths are completely positive, nor are all weaknesses necessarily detrimental to the library. You will find there are many ways to develop an effective marketing plan, based on both the strengths and the weaknesses of your library.

Once you have identified your library's strengths and weaknesses, determine how they will affect your marketing plan. Weigh the pros and cons of each item as you begin the planning process. Each situation must be analyzed to determine where attention should be focused.

Example: Library X has a staff that is composed of recent hires.

Strength	Weakness
New ideas	Unfamiliar with collection
New skills	Unfamiliar with community
Change agents	May change too rapidly

On the one hand, having recently hired staff could be viewed as a strength because there are new employees with new ideas and skill sets who are ready to make changes. This same situation could also be viewed as a weakness because newer staff might not be as familiar with the collection or with the people in that community, and too many changes might have an adverse effect on users.

It may help to identify the cause of each weakness through the use of an environmental scan. Look beyond specific library factors to other factors that affect the business of the library. For instance, the reasons why the library's budget was cut could include the following:

- Businesses have left, so the tax base is not as great as it had been.
- People are purchasing eBooks rather than downloading eBooks from the library or coming to the library
- Users don't know that they can borrow eBooks and other e-resources from the library.
- Users are not aware that the library can obtain books for them even if those books are not in the library's catalog.

Now let's take a look at *opportunities*. Opportunities may not always be readily apparent, so you need to be creative in your assessment of the situation.

Example: Library X has a staff that is composed of many recent hires.

Strength	Weakness	Opportunity	Threat
New ideas and skills	Unfamiliar with collection and community	Begin mentoring new staff to develop collection, programs, and services and introduce them to local constituencies	Resentment among new staff and continuing staff members
		Begin to record library's history through policies and procedures or an oral history	Organization's "memory" may be lost
Change agents	May change too rapidly	Host all-staff and volunteer retreat to begin strategic plan assessment	Senior staff may be overruled

As another example, your library could have an opportunity to overcome a weakness such as lack of community use by informing the community of library services, programs, and collections. The marketing plan will then include ways in which the community will be informed about library activities.

Let's look at one more example of opportunities. A library that experienced a disaster that destroyed much of its collection and displaced staff from their offices could identify the following internal and external opportunities:

- Internal:
    - Assess needs of users to assist with collection replacement and development
    - Expand digital collection and utilize space for community activities
    - Strengthen communication channels within organization

- External:
    - Work with outside partners in community to plan for improvements in collection and building
    - Develop grant proposals to improve collection and building

Now that you've thought about the strengths, weaknesses, and opportunities in your library, it's time to address *threats*. These are impediments to the programs and services of the library. They focus on an area of library service and the environmental factors that affect that area. Following are examples of threats:

- A public library's video collection could be threatened by the increased use of online streaming videos sources like Netflix.
- Library usage can be threatened by the increased use of information technology or mobile devices. You can turn this potential threat into an opportunity by promoting the value-added services that are available in your library. Develop a ROI (return on investment) campaign or offer workshops on new technologies.

Example: Library X has a staff that is composed of many recent hires

Strength	Weakness	Opportunity	Threat
New ideas and skills	Unfamiliar with collection and community	Begin mentoring new staff to develop collection, programs, and services and introduce them to local constituencies	Resentment among new staff and continuing staff members
		Begin to record library's history through policies and procedures or an oral history	Organization's "memory" may be lost
Change agents	May change too rapidly	Host all-staff and volunteer retreat to begin strategic plan assessment	Senior staff may be overruled

The SWOT analysis is an especially useful tool for libraries. However, you need to decide which types of data collection method and analysis are best suited for your particular situation. The next section discusses how to ascertain which tools will make the best use of your library's resources, so that you can successfully analyze your community's needs and develop an appropriate marketing plan.

Deciding What Method(s) to Use

The data collection method and analysis you choose are based on the information you need to get from the library's users or nonusers. They also depend on the amount of time and the resources available to you. Starting questions to gather the information you need about the community so that you can develop a strong marketing plan might be, "How long will it take to collect the data, and how much time and money do I have to analyze the data?" Following are possible answers:

- Time and money to get all of the answers are no object!
- Some time and some money are available to get answers.
- Are you kidding? I needed this last week, and there is no money.

Your data collection will be driven by how you answer those questions. Let's take a closer look at the possible responses.

Abundant Time and Money

Although the last answer is a common response from most librarians, we'll start with the first one. Let's suppose you have time and money available so you can hire a consulting firm or bring in a consultant to assess the library and the community of users and nonusers. Consultants develop assessment tools, gather and analyze data, and report the results. If you don't know how to find a consultant, you might find a local educational institution whose faculty and students will create and conduct your survey. You could participate in studies such as LibQUAL™, a proprietary service from the Association of Research Libraries, which provides librarians with ways to assess their services as they prepare for planning and marketing.

Consultants or consulting agencies are a luxury that can be used in some library situations. When information derived from data collection and analysis is a high priority for the planning process, funds may be available. If you are able to hire a consultant, you will need to understand the variety of survey methods available. For more information about survey methods, see the "Gathering Data about Your Community" section of this chapter.

It's likely, however, that you won't be able to hire a consultant to perform your data collection and analysis for you. Let's look at some other alternatives, if you have some time and some money.

Some Time and Some Money

"Some time and some money" is a very realistic response for many librarians. Following are some suggested procedures for librarians who have some lead time and a budget allocation, even if it is just a small amount of money:

- Search the literature for surveys that address the issues of concern to you.
- Assess the pros and cons of the different survey formats in regard to time and costs for data collection and analysis:
  - Oral—by telephone or in person
  - Print—by mail, in the library, or off-site
  - Electronic
- Conduct the survey and prepare for data analysis prior to completion. Then assess the information derived from the survey and make an informed decision.
- Set up focus groups.

With these resources you have some flexibility. Choose the method that fits your time and budget allocation and make it work for you!

No Time and No Money

Librarians who are in a hurry and have no budget might try the following:

- Implement the NGT with staff and volunteers.
- Use the NGT with a local group of library users or nonusers.
  - Librarians should be connected to the community at large through membership in associations or committees.
- Do a literature review to determine if needed information exists.
  - Networking: Call colleagues in similar libraries to ask about their experiences.
  - Meet with established Friends of the Library groups (see Chapter 5 for details) to seek their advice.
  - Check studies that contain data relevant to your needs. Potential sources include:
      census data to understand demographic changes in the community,

      studies conducted in the community, and

      national studies.
- Study in-house statistics for circulation, door counts, and electronic usage for regular service or events.

You can use any combination of the data collection and analysis methods described in this chapter to determine which library services best meet your community's needs. Be creative! The goal is to get the information needed to create an effective marketing plan.

Putting It All Together

If public librarians are interested in promoting resources and services to their users, they might ask the community the following questions:

- What kinds of factors do you think will affect library usage?
- Why would you want or not want to use the library?

Following are possible responses that could affect your library use:

- Need to use the library for research or study.
- Use the library computers for job searches, social networking, or other.
- No knowledge of how to use reference resources; the library is an intimidating place.
- Music, food, and drink are/are not allowed in the library.
- Hours are convenient/inconvenient.
- Location is convenient/inconvenient.
- Furniture is comfortable/uncomfortable.
- Librarians are helpful/unhelpful.
- Librarians are friendly/unfriendly.
- Resources are available/unavailable.
- Library is attractive/unattractive.

Using this list of items important to library patrons, you can assess the internal strengths of the library. You could conclude that the library has a pleasant atmosphere, comfortable chairs, plenty of workstations, and extensive hours; is accessible to the community; and has excellent print and electronic resources, including a great selection of full-text databases. A SWOT analysis might indicate that in spite of these strengths, the library has significant weaknesses: underutilization and patron dissatisfaction.

The next step for the librarian is to decide how to utilize these strengths and weaknesses to optimize new marketing opportunities to prevent the threat of potential budget cuts due to under-usage. Before you can plan a course of action, you need to find information about your users. You can't just assume that you know what they are thinking. Sometimes you can guess correctly, but there's no sense wasting time and money on your marketing activities unless you have some concrete data to ensure that you will achieve the desired results.

Following are some ways to use planning techniques to handle this situation and to market the library:

- Develop a focus group composed of patrons to determine which of the following is the best way to reach them and promote the library's resources:
  - website
  - social media
  - brochure
  - e-mail
  - newspaper ads
  - posters
  - raffle or giveaway (T-shirts, flash drives, etc.)
- Develop a survey to determine
  - why patrons use or do not use the library and
  - whether patrons know about the resources available to them.
- Promote the electronic databases and other e-resources, *and* how they can be used by patrons, *and* how to use them.

The next chapter discusses how to create a marketing plan. It also covers how to evaluate marketing projects. If you're going to spend time, money, and effort creating and implementing a marketing plan, you want to know whether you've done a good job, so that you can emulate the plan the next time around or make changes if it wasn't so successful.

The rest of the book discusses public relations, working with the press, and how to use different media to appeal to various groups. Fund-raising and development are also covered, because they have become more of a necessity in all types of libraries and also fall under the topic of marketing. There's certainly much to learn about marketing, but let's take it one step at a time! In Chapter 2 we begin the marketing plan.

Resources to Consult for Community Analysis and Strategic Planning

- Strategic planning
  - The October 2012 issue of *Feliciter* (vol. 58, no. 5) is focused on strategic planning. The articles provide useful and humorous approaches to environmental scanning and strategic planning; see http://www.cla.ca/feliciter/2012/58–5/index .html.
- Census data
  - Comparison of public libraries; see https://harvester.census.gov/imls/compare/.
  - Community data: American Fact Finder based on U.S. census data; see http:// factfinder2.census.gov/faces/nav/jsf/pages/index.xhtml.

- OCLC WebJunction©; see http://webjunction.org/explore-topics.html.
  - Planning and coordination

- DAZL Digital Arizona Libraries Report and Environmental Scan: http://evoke.cvlsites.org/resources-guides-and-more/digital-arizona-library-environmental-scan/.
- NGT sources
  - Gaining Consensus Among Stakeholders Through the Nominal Group Technique: http://www.cdc.gov/healthyyouth/evaluation/pdf/brief7.pdf.
  - University of Illinois Extension: http://www.communitydevelopment.uiuc.edu/sp/Step5/Nominal%20Group%20Technique.pdf.
  - *Journal of Extension*: http://www.joe.org/joe/1984march/iw2.php.

Chapter 2

Develop a Marketing Plan

After completing the planning process, it's time to develop your marketing plan. You can think of the marketing plan as a map: You've decided what your goal should be (what services and programs your library would like to market), and now it's time to figure out how to get there. Your marketing plan will outline the best and most efficient way of reaching that goal.

The marketing plan is an organizational tool. It allows you to make targeted decisions about your marketing ideas and then helps you organize and implement these ideas. It also makes the entire staff aware of the library's marketing goals and the process to follow to reach them.

The last chapter presented a library that would like to increase the number of preschool children and their caregivers who come into the library. Since this goal was in line with the library's strategic plan, the library staff researched the community and then came up with ideas for ways to market the library's services, collection, and programming to current and potential patrons. These marketing ideas will be the foundation for the library's marketing plan. The plan itself will lay out the process of implementing these strategies to get to the end result: raising awareness about library services and attracting preschool children and their caregivers to the library.

This chapter introduces the basic components of a marketing plan. It takes an in-depth look at each of these components so that you can create a marketing plan for your own library, followed by examples of marketing plans that have been constructed by various libraries. It's important to look at marketing plans from many sources, since there are many formats for these plans. You can decide which format works best for you and your library.

Marketing Plan Components

Although marketing plans can follow various formats, almost all plans include the following components:

- an executive summary,
- an environmental scan,
- marketing goals and objectives,
- a marketing plan and strategy,
- an action plan,
- a budget, and
- an evaluation.

Let's take a look at each of these components.

The Executive Summary

The executive summary is the global overview of everything that will be presented in the marketing plan. It can be used for two purposes:

- as an introduction to the marketing plan itself, or
- as an overview of the marketing plan to be presented for funding or approval from another authority.

Although the executive summary appears first in the marketing plan, it will actually be written last, since it is a reflection of everything that occurs in the plan. As you read the description of the marketing plan, don't worry if you're not sure exactly what to include. It should become apparent after you create the rest of your plan.

Introduction to Your Organization

At the beginning of the executive summary, you should introduce your organization, especially if the summary will be read by someone outside the library. Give highlights of your library. For example, if your library has an interesting history, include information about it. You might also want to talk about the strengths of your collection, staff, programs, and services. Think about the SWOT (strengths, weaknesses, opportunities, threats) analysis discussed in Chapter 1. What strengths did you determine were a part of your library? Include those in the executive summary, if they're relevant.

If you already have a boilerplate that you use for library marketing materials, you can use it in the executive summary. A *boilerplate* is a standard—and brief—description of your library that can be used for a number of different purposes. It gathers statistics about your library (usage, strengths of the collection, etc.) and explains the importance and relevance of the library, the collection, and the staff. If you don't already have a boilerplate, you should create one and keep it up to date. (An example is provided in Appendix B.) You will use the information in your boilerplate to write a grant proposal or an executive summary. While we're on the subject, you should also prepare an "elevator speech" about your library to have on hand when the need arises. Let's say you're in an elevator and the president of a company that you would like to get funding from happens to be in the elevator with you. Are you going to stand there and look at the floor that whole time, or are you going to make your point because you have that person as a captive audience? You want to market your library! If you have memorized the relevant points that you want to say, you can be ready in a minute to give your speech. Just give the highlights and any relevant statistics. Here's an example: "I'd like to take this opportunity to tell you about an exciting project that we're trying to get underway at the library. And did you know our library serves 500 children and their parents?" Prepare what you'd want to say to people if you had their attention for two minutes, the time it takes to go up in an elevator. And then have extra things to say in case the elevator gets stuck! Some of the statements you use in your elevator speech can also be used in your executive summary.

Mission Statement and Goals and Objectives

In your executive summary you may also include your library's mission statement and its goals and objectives. These may be imported from the strategic plan, if your library has one. If it doesn't, don't worry. Just think about your library's goals and list them clearly. Remember that your marketing plan should be aligned with the library's broader goals, so you've probably already outlined these objectives for yourself. Include them, in a clear and concise way, in the executive summary.

List of the People Involved in the Marketing Plan

Your executive summary should also include a list of those who are going to be involved in the marketing project. You don't have to list every person who works in the library, but you should highlight the key players. For instance, if your marketing plan is aimed at bringing preschool children to the library, you would say in the executive summary that the youth or children's librarian will be a part of the project. You should identify any others in the cast of characters and, if you think it's necessary, briefly explain the structure of your organization. Explain the major points of your plan, although not in detail, since the detail comes later in the plan.

Summary of the Marketing Objectives and Recommended Strategies

The executive summary is a power-packed statement that identifies your marketing need. It should be no more than two pages long and, with careful writing, you can get it down to one page. Remember that it's an overview. Since you may be giving it out to a number of different people, you don't want it bogged down with extraneous information. Again, the executive summary comes first, but it isn't written until the very end.

The Environmental Scan

In this section you should outline the results of the environmental scan (discussed in Chapter 1). This section does not have to be long; just provide information about your location, your target market, and the competitive environment. Also, you should identify any key issues that your organization faces.

Marketing Goals and Objectives

In this section you should state your marketing goals and objectives, which are an essential part of your marketing plan. If you think of your marketing plan as a map for a successful marketing campaign, the goal is the destination and the objectives are the landmarks along the way. You're not going to vary from the route that you've set up.

The marketing goal, then, is the major thing you want to accomplish in your marketing campaign, such as increasing awareness of your product among your target audience. It could be one thing or more than one. The marketing objectives follow the goal; these are the steps you will follow to reach the goal and complete the marketing plan. They are also what you use to measure whether you have reached your goal.

In our example, the library's goal is to get more parents and caregivers to know about the library's programs, resources, and collections for preschool children. The objectives for the library might be to increase story-hour attendance and increase circulation of preschool-age materials.

You should also include in this section the time frame for achieving your marketing objectives. That way, you'll have a path to follow when using your marketing plan.

The Marketing Plan and Strategy

The strategy is your game plan for achieving your marketing objectives. It is essentially the heart of your marketing plan and covers the four "Ps" of marketing:

> **P**roduct
>
> **P**rice
>
> **P**romotion
>
> **P**lace

This method has been developed for the profit sector, but you can modify it for your library.

Let's take a look at the first "P": *product.* Describe your library's product or service in detail. Don't forget to include its features and benefits. Just because you're not actually selling something doesn't mean that you don't have anything to offer your community. Perhaps you are implementing a new service or building a new collection. Or maybe you now have many more board books for babies in your collection, which should appeal to new parents.

The second "P" is *price.* How much will this service or product cost, and how will it be funded? The service probably won't cost your user anything, but it will cost you and your library time and effort. You must ask yourself if you will incur some real costs associated with your production, perhaps a mailing. You also have to figure out how much staff time the service will take, since this is also a real cost. When we discuss the budget later in this chapter, you'll have a better idea of the costs of your marketing project. Since budgets are tight in so many institutions, you'll need to think about how your plan will be funded. Will the money come from your regular budget, or are you going to ask somebody for money for this project? If you plan to ask for money, take a look at our chapter on fund-raising.

Now let's talk about the third "P": *promotion.* Describe the promotional tools or tactics you'll use to accomplish your marketing objectives. This is an especially important part of the marketing plan, because even if you have a fabulous program, no one will come if they don't know about it. In this section you should cover how you're going to promote your product or service. Remember that an important part of promotion is making clear to potential users how your program will benefit them. If you're trying to get preschool children and their caregivers into your library, you need to make it clear to the caregivers that your program will benefit their children.

Place is the fourth "P." Most likely your marketing program will occur in your library. But perhaps there's a better place to host your event, like outside or at a community center. Think about what will be the best place for users to access your service. If the product will be held in the library, where will you hold it? If it's a display, will you display it in a glass case? Would an online display work?

The Action Plan

The action plan section is your marketing "to do" list. It includes an outline of specific tasks and describes what will be done, when each task will begin or be completed, who will accomplish the tasks, and the resources assigned to the project. This is one of the most important sections of the plan, and it needs to be thought out in advance, although many librarians don't do so. However, creating an action plan, and following through with it, will save a lot of time and trouble later and will help you avoid any unpleasant surprises. You don't want to find out too late that you hadn't considered everything and the costs have become prohibitive.

Although this sounds like what is more formally called "project management," it isn't that elaborate. Just look at what needs to be accomplished and think about the best way to do it. For example, if you were going to hold an early childhood program, you may want to hold the event before the library usually opens so that the librarian is not distracted by other patrons needing help.

Think about every aspect of the program, including the work before the event and after it. Figure out how to promote your service or product: Who's going to write the press release? Who's going to notify the media? Who's going to handle the social media? The other thing to think about is how to capture the event for later records. Will someone take pictures or record it? Make sure that your program is captured so that the pictures can go on your social media sites immediately after (or even during!) the event and later in your newsletter or your annual report.

The Budget

In this section, list the cost of the marketing activities you are describing in the rest of the marketing plan. Your obvious costs are staff time, printing, and publication costs, but there may be hidden costs as well.

You should pay attention to staff costs, because if a staff member is in charge of the program, that person may not be able to perform his or her regular duties. Will you have to bring in somebody else to run the program or help in the library? What are the real costs associated with this? If it's going to take someone 50 hours to do the program, how much would 50 hours' worth of salary and benefits be?

You're also most likely going to have to print up things like promotional materials and handouts. Even if you're doing the printing in-house, there's a cost associated with the paper and the photocopying. If you decide to set up a website or to use social media, that's going to cost in terms of people who will do it, unless you have volunteers. However, even using volunteers has a certain cost because someone at your library will have to oversee their instruction and engage in a certain amount of monitoring their progress.

If you've ever written a grant proposal for funds, you may begin to see that there is not much difference between that and a marketing plan. Many of the components are similar. If you have the basic skills for strategic planning and writing a grant, you have a head start on preparing a marketing plan. These skills come into play over and over again in a library. If you learned strategic planning and how to write a grant proposal, you can certainly draw on that experience when thinking about the budget for your marketing project.

The Evaluation

An important part of the marketing plan is the evaluation section. Evaluation is built into the marketing plan at the beginning and should be decided on before, not after, the program begins. You need to set up in advance your measures for success. They're really nobody else's measures but your own, but you want to know if you have reached your target goal, fallen short, or exceeded it. For every part of your plan, you should set up some measure by which to assess it. A measure may simply be comparing the number of people you would like to attend the program to the number who actually do, or it could be the number of articles about the program that appear in the newspaper, on the radio, or in other media. You might also see how many times a post is "liked" on Facebook or "retweeted" on Twitter. Following are some other ideas for how to measure and evaluate your program:

- Use circulation statistics.
- Count the amount of money raised.
- Count the number of people getting new library cards.
- Do door counts.
- Count the number of website hits.
- Count the number of items (like coffee mugs) purchased.
- Do a survey of people who attended the program.

Remember that it's okay if you fall short of your goal; you can always learn from your mistakes. It's better to have a measure and realize that you didn't meet it, rather than saying, "Oh, this was a great success" when it truly wasn't. Of course, if you do better than you expected, a measure also allows you to say, "The program exceeded our expectations."

Examples of Marketing Plans

The marketing plan described in this chapter is a classic textbook example. You don't have to follow this plan exactly, but it's critical that you decide at the beginning what components you will include in the plan and in what order they will appear. Once you have done a few plans and are familiar with the process, you can get them done very quickly, but your first one may take some time. It doesn't have to be overly elaborate; it just needs to include the appropriate information. If you're fortunate enough to be in a library that has its own marketing team, your marketing plan may be more involved. But chances are you're going to be doing marketing in addition to budget, reference, and whatever else you have to do to keep your library running. So it's critical that you become familiar with the format of the plan so that you can create it very quickly.

To get some ideas of great marketing plans, look at the John Cotton Dana Library Public Relations awards. Winners are listed in Appendix D. These awards are given by the American Library Association (ALA), the H.W. Wilson Foundation, and EBSCO every year and are a competition of librarians and their libraries. They develop marketing projects and plans over the course of a year and then submit them to a committee. This committee selects the best from all different types of libraries. The actual awards are presented at a ceremony during ALA's conference each year. If you would like to see examples of these marketing projects, visit the website at http://www.ebscohost.com/academic/john-cotton-dana.

Another example of a marketing plan from the Hood River County Library in Oregon provides you with an idea of the scope and length of a marketing plan; see http://www. ebscohost.com/resources/john-cotton-dana/winners/2013/hood-river-county-library-district. pdf. In 2010, Hood River County Library (Oregon) district closed due to lack of funding, but through a taxpayer initiative and an effective and creative marketing plan the library reimagined its services, increased usage, and won a John Cotton Dana Award. These links to public board meetings indicate the type of environmental scanning and planning that is needed in the development of a marketing plan: http://www.hoodriver.plinkit.org/files/board/agendas/2012–13/packet_2012–10–17.pdf and http://www.hoodriver.plinkit.org/files/board/minutes/2011–12/Minutes%202011–11–17.pdf.

Other marketing plans can be found in the resources listed in Appendix E, and also look at the examples in Appendix F.

The next chapter discusses how to use media, newsletters, and annual reports to communicate your library's programs and services to the community.

Chapter 3

Communicate to the Community: Using the Media, Newsletters, and Annual Reports to Market the Library

Libraries should be in the public eye all the time, and it is important to be as visible as possible without spending lots of money on printing and mailing materials. Social media is an effective marketing tool that will be discussed in a separate chapter. This chapter focuses on access to the community through local media outlets. Most communities have a local newspaper and community website, and many have local radio and television stations, all of which are used by the community to get information. Each of these media outlets is always looking for information that will be of interest to the community. Since the library's resources and programs are offered to community members, the media are usually happy to help get the word out about library activities. Having the media do that for the library is effective in terms of the time, money, and effort saved and in the size of the audience that is reached.

To make the most out of your local media outlets, you need to come up with a *media plan*. The first step in developing the media plan is to determine

- how to get information about your library out to the community (printing, mailing, electronic distribution, using traditional media and social media);
- what kind of information should be sent out (programming information, new books and services, bond election information, new personnel, fund-raising information);
- how you are going to distribute the information in advance (instead of just flying around at the last minute trying to figure out who's going to get the information!); and
- when you want to use the media, and how often.

As you think about how to distribute information about your library, you need to decide what kinds of publicity can be handled by the library and what should be handled by local media outlets.

A number of marketing tools are available that you and other librarians may use, including the following:

- Personal contact with users/nonusers (e-mail address, snail-mail address, phone number)
- Internet: web page, electronic bulletin board, blogs
- Social Media (discussed in Chapter 4)
- Word of mouth
- In-house displays
- Flyers, bookmarks, ads, or coupons that can be placed in
  - books as they circulate,
  - utility bills,
  - local publications,
  - public offices and organizations,
  - school mailings, and
  - organizational publications (school, church, or community newsletters).

The following marketing tools can be used by the media:

- Upcoming programs/calendars of events (summer reading, book discussions, public lectures)
- New materials (weekly book reviews or new acquisitions)
- Feature stories (ways in which the library or librarians have influenced a person or event)

This chapter covers how your library can develop a plan to work with the media. We show you how to create a media list and how to contact the people who are on your list. Then you'll learn how to create a press release, public service announcement (PSA), press kit, and calendar of events. Finally, we give you some useful sources of information that can help your library when working with the media.

Creating a Media List

The first step in creating a media plan is to develop a media list that identifies the newspaper, radio, and television reporters who will publicize information about your library. The list only needs to be created once, but it should be updated by staff members on a regular (at least yearly) basis.

To create your media list, first identify all the local media outlets in your community, such as

- newspapers,
- radio stations,
- television stations,
- websites,
- school newspapers,
- church bulletins, and
- community center newsletters.

Next, identify the appropriate contact person and contact information for each of these media outlets. Remember to get the following information:

- Name
- Position
- Address
- Phone number
- Fax number
- E-mail address

As you gather this information, it's important to call the organization, rather than rely on information posted on a website. Websites are not always reliable, and this kind of information can change quickly. It is important to identify the person who currently has the responsibilities, rather than the person who was the contact two years ago.

Contacting People on Your Media List

Getting to Know You

Once you have compiled your media list, contact each person on the list. This should be done before you actually need someone to advertise your library's program. Marketing is communication, and you should form a relationship with these media representatives so that they can help you when you need them. After all, wouldn't you much rather talk to somebody you already know?

Here are some things to remember when contacting a media representative:

- Contact the media representative *before* you need him or her.
- Send a letter or e-mail of introduction.
- Follow up with a phone call.
- Do not chat about the weather:
    - have a succinct list of what you want the person to know about your library,
    - find out what he or she is interested in covering, and
    - determine his or her publishing deadlines.

Getting to Know You Better

Once you have introduced yourself to a media representative, it's time to get to know him or her even better. It's important that you make these representatives feel that you are out for their best interest. If you do this, they will want to cover your library. Following are some things that you need to find out from your media representatives:

- How they prefer to get updates about your library:
    - Press release via e-mail, fax, or mail
    - Phone calls
- How much lead time they need (a month, a week, a day)

Be sure to add all of this information to your media list!

One great way to get to know your media representatives better is to invite them to visit your library. Extend an invitation to individual representatives to visit the library on different days in order for them to get to know you and the organization and to showcase the exciting and innovative programs in your library. Or, you could just invite the representative to visit on a regular day so that you can talk to and show him the resources and services that are provided.

One thing to remember when you invite media representatives to your library: the photographer won't necessarily come with the interviewer and may not come at all. Have some photos ready to give the interviewer. You may want to find out before the interviewer comes if there are specifications for photos—either print or digital. You may also want to keep a list of photographers in your media list, so that you can call on them if needed.

It also occasionally happens that media representatives say they're coming to cover a special event, and then something happens and they don't arrive. They're probably still interested in your event, so your library needs to provide information that the media outlet can use to cover your program. Some of the methods for doing this are press releases, PSAs, press kits, a calendar of events, and your annual report. You can also post information about each event using the Web and social media, and you can provide information to the representative on where to access the most recent updates.

The Press Release

The first media material you'll probably create is a press release. This is a concise document that includes relevant information about your library's new program or service. It should contain precise information with an interesting title that catches the interest of your media representative.

It is important that the press releases that you send are newsworthy in order to establish your credibility with the media reps. They will become accustomed to knowing that you only provide them with relevant stories. If you send press releases for inconsequential events or acquisitions, they will be ignored. So make sure that when you send a press release, it really is of value.

All the pertinent facts should be included in the first paragraph of the press release, and the entire document should be no longer than one or two pages. A person reading a press release usually reads quickly, looking just for the facts. For this reason, the press release must attract the person's attention, and include the pertinent information. Here are some things to remember when writing a press release:

- Include only one or two pages that give all the pertinent details.
- The title should be informative and attention-getting.
- The first paragraph should include a brief overview of interest, and it must cover the who, what, when, where, and why details.
- Stick to the facts.
- Include the library's contact information.
- Include in the last paragraph a boilerplate about the library.

The boilerplate in the very last paragraph should include something interesting about your library that you'd like people to know. It's a final reminder that includes relevant information about your library that you want the reader to remember.

The press release has to have a standard look to it so that people know it's coming from you. Make sure your library's logo or branding is at the top of the document. Always include the date on the press release, so that media representatives know when the information should be released to the public. Then always provide the contact person, telephone number, and e-mail address, so that if there are any questions, the media representative will be able to go directly to the person in the library who has the information he or she is looking for.

There are other press release standards. At the bottom of the page you should write "for more information" and provide your contact information. At the end of the release put either three pound/number symbols (# # #) or hyphen-30-hyphen (-30-). If you are going onto two pages, at the end of the first page put the word "more" so that the reader knows there's more on the next page.

The Public Service Announcement

Another kind of media material is the PSA. It is a short announcement that can be read on radio or television in 10-, 30-, or 60-second spots. Often PSAs come on in the early morning on an obscure television station. Nevertheless, you never know who's going to see a PSA, so your library should use PSAs if possible.

To write a PSA, you first need to determine what spots are available. Call people on your media list to see if they have space for PSAs and how long they are. Once you know how much time you have for your PSA, you can write it. Make sure you don't include too much information, because you don't want the announcer to speed-read it. You do need to get the pertinent information at the beginning and end of the announcement, because people tend to remember what they hear first and last. Have you ever noticed how in radio announcements they repeat a phone number several times? Various studies indicate that people need to hear something seven to twenty times before they remember it, so make sure the information in your PSA is simple and repeatable. A template for your PSA follows.

Public Service Announcement Template

[Library Logo/Branding: Top of the Page]

[Contact Person Name]

[Contact Person Telephone Number]

[Contact Person Fax Number]

[Contact Person E-mail Address]

[Title of Public Service Announcement]

[Approximate Length of PSA]

[Write the text of your PSA here. Remember to keep it simple and repeatable. Don't forget to include the contact information!]

The Press Kit

A press kit is a folder that contains marketing materials about a speaker or event being held in the library. It can be given to media outlets before the event so that they have background information about and photos of the person who will be speaking or the event that will be taking place. For instance, if an author were going to speak at your library, the press kit might include his or her biography, a list of published works, and a photo of that person. You would also include information about your library.

While some press kits can be very involved (especially those from vendors), you don't have to spend a lot of money to create one. The most simple is just a regular folder that you can get for a dollar. Then just print up copies of information that you want the media to know. Put in a brochure for something that's going on or include your annual report or monthly newspaper.

Press kits are a great way to communicate with people on your media list. You may want to have an interview and say that the speaker will be available to the media at a particular time, or you may just want to contact one media representative and say, "I will make this author available to you exclusively." Doing so may sweeten the pot a little bit. You're taking a chance, but if you have established a relationship with your media reps, you'd be surprised at how grateful they may be.

The Calendar of Events

A simple way to advertise programs and events in your library is to post them in a calendar of events. Often local newspapers publish a weekly or monthly calendar. Television and radio stations sometimes have community calendars that they post on their websites or announce over the air. Contact the media outlets on your list to see if they have any type of calendar where you can post your library events.

The Annual Report

Annual reports are compilations of circulation statistics, reference statistics, budget allocations, and. . . . Wait a minute! No, they're not!!! Annual reports should be the crown jewel in your marketing array of publications. The annual report should be used to highlight the success experienced at your library during the previous year. The publication can be sent to:

- the board of directors,
- elected officials in the community,
- real estate offices/Welcome Wagon,
- library donors,
- day care centers,
- senior centers,
- community centers, and
- others.

The report can be made available in print or electronic formats. Print formats can be published in a variety of ways:

- on standard 8-1/2-by-11-inch, 8-1/2-by-14-inch, or 11-by-17-inch paper;
- in a tabloid, booklet, trifold, or poster format;
- on glossy, colored, or white paper; and
- in just black, four-color, or single-color type.

Some libraries have produced coffee-table quality annual reports that have been funded by a donor or institution. Perhaps the local bank or grocery store would underwrite the annual report in exchange for recognition in the publication. The Mt. Lebanon Public Library in Pennsylvania has "published" its annual report on 5-by-7-inch notepads produced by a local printer. The library's contact information and a different fact about the library are printed on each page.

Examples showing the creative use of text, photographs, and graphics in annual reports are included in Appendix H. Think beyond the stuffy report when you produce your next annual report. Use the report as an opportunity to showcase the library's accomplishments.

Newsletters

Newsletters are an effective way for libraries to communicate with their community of users and nonusers. Newsletters may be produced in-house or with a commercial vendor or they may be electronic. Newsletter content may focus on upcoming or past events, new acquisitions, a list of donors, and feature stories. A calendar of events is a popular section of most library newsletters.

While it may be costly in terms of staff time and effort and printing and mailing, the benefits of a newsletter are innumerable, including

- distribution and promotion of a calendar of events,
- a focus on new materials or resources,
- features about topics of interest to community members,
- showing support from the community, and
- providing evidence of activities to library funders.

Newsletters can be very effective even if they are not filled with color photos and graphics. Knowing basic design principles can help you produce an in-house publication that is helpful in making your community aware of the library.

As you prepare to create your newsletter, you will have to make some decisions. The steps involved are discussed below.

Step 1: Why Does My Library Need a Newsletter?

The first question you need to answer is why your library needs a newsletter. You must have a compelling reason to publish a newsletter and a list of what you want to include in each issue. If you have decided you definitely wish to publish a newsletter, here are some items you might want to include in it:

- a calendar of events,
- highlights of new items in the collection,
- thanks to donors,
- a showcase of past events,
- contact information and directions to the library,
- materials to reach current library users, and
- materials to reach potential library users.

Step 2: Who Will Develop the Newsletter?

The next question concerns the production of the newsletter. Who will be responsible for writing the content and doing the design and layout? Are there staff members or volunteers who have the time and ability to complete it in a timely manner? Once you make the decision to publish a newsletter, you need to ensure that it will be ready on time. What will be included in the newsletter?

- Identify the person(s) responsible for these functions:
  - selecting content,
  - writing and editing, and
  - doing the design and layout.
- Create a library brand and establish a template (see example below) for the newsletter.

Step 3: When and Where Will the Newsletter Be Published?

Decide how often the newsletter should be published and how much it will cost. Do you have the time, money, and material to produce the newsletter on a monthly, quarterly, or semiannual basis?

- Will the newsletter be produced in hard copy?
  - Will it be available in the library?
  - Will it be available in other locations—grocery stores, community centers?

- Will it be mailed?
    - Will it be mailed to library card holders?
    - Will it be mailed to nonlibrary card holders?
- Will it be available electronically on your website?
- What will the costs be for
    - producing it,
    - printing it,
    - mailing it, or
    - publishing it electronically?
- Will it be produced
    - monthly,
    - quarterly,
    - semiannually, or
    - at some other frequency?

Step 4: Determining Costs—Printing and Mailing Considerations

Follow the steps indicated for whichever format you choose:

- Printing
    - Decide how many newsletters you will need to have printed.
    - Decide whether the newsletter will be black and white or color. (Many color options are available, so check with your local printer. You may opt to use one color on the front and back pages so that the charge will be less than for using one or more colors on each page.)
    - Will it be printed in-house or commercially?
    - What size will the paper be?
    - What type of paper will be used (glossy, color, newsprint, recycled, etc.)?
    - Decide how many copies will be mailed.

        What are the costs to obtain mailing labels?

        What are the costs for postage?
    - Negotiate with a local printing company for an annual contract.
- Electronic
    - Decide whether the newsletter will be available in print *and* electronic versions *or* electronic only.
    - How will the e-newsletter be distributed? Will it be accessible on the website sent or via e-mail to library users? Who will prepare the electronic version?

> ## Newsletter Template
>
> - Logo/brand: Determine the "look" that the library wants to project. It can be an established or a new logo. Select the following:
>   - Type font that will be used in each newsletter
>   - Paper
>
>   White, color, recycled, newsprint
>
>   Size: 8-1/2-by-11, 8-1/2-by-14, 11-by-17, or other
>   - Color of ink
> - Content:
>   - Contact information
>   - Calendar of events
>   - New acquisitions
>   - Photo gallery of events
>
>   Speakers
>
>   Programs
>
>   National Library Week
>
>   "Teen Tech Week"
>
>   Summer reading
>
>   Clubs
>
>   Other
>   - Special columns
>
>   Fun facts
>
>   Local history
>
>   Technology updates
>
>   Other
>   - Honor roll of library donors

Many sources are available to help you develop successful newsletters. Sample newsletters can be seen in Appendix I.

Handling Bad Press

Before ending this chapter, we want to address how you might consider handling bad press before it occurs. In the event of bad press, you should have a person in the library who is designated as the contact for the media. This person should be the official spokesperson for the library in order to project the information approved by the director or the library board. This is to ensure that the correct messages—and not conflicting information—are being provided to the media. You should instruct all other staff members to direct media representatives to that person, if their questions are about something that's affecting the library. A response to bad press doesn't always have to be immediate; you can simply say that a statement will be released or you will talk to the media at a specific time. That way, the library has a chance to prepare what it would like to convey to the media. Remember that bad press isn't always such an awful thing, because sometimes you can make it into lemonade and turn the situation around.

Useful Sources

When working with media, you can draw from many useful sources. This section lists some of them to provide an idea of what's out there. The American Library Association (ALA), the Association of Research Libraries, and the Medical Library Association all have good, practical, downloadable sites.

American Library Association

Public Awareness Tools and Resources, http://www.ala.org/advocacy/advleg/public awareness/campaign%40yourlibrary/prtools

Communications Handbook, http://www.ala.org/advocacy/sites/ala.org.advocacy/ files/content/advleg/advocacyuniversity/advclearinghouse/commhandbook.pdf

Media Relations Handbook, http://www.ala.org/advocacy/advleg/publicawareness/ca mpaign%40yourlibrary/prtools/handbook

The ALA has excellent materials for working with the media. In particular, you should look at their *Media Relations Handbook for Libraries*. It includes an introductory letter for libraries, which can be customized and sent to your local media outlets. The handbook also gives you information on what media attention can do for the library and tells you how to approach and engage the media. A variety of tools are provided to pitch stories to media representatives that will get visibility for your library.

Media opportunities exist for human interest or feature articles as well as library programs or events. You might also consider writing a letter to the editor of a local publication about something that is happening at your library or provide a regular column to the publication. Both of these activities serve to publicize your library.

Medical Library Association

Making a Difference: Media Relations, http://www.mlanet.org/publications/tool_kit/ media_relate.html

The Medical Library Association, although you may not ordinarily think of it as a resource for public libraries, also has useful media hints. "Making a Difference: Media Relations" is a long toolkit on how to develop fact sheets to work with the media, develop photographs and graphics for the media, and write a photo caption. They also give advice about creating a media list and other media materials. Their suggestions could easily be adapted for your library. If you have little funding, you may be interested in a list of free items.

Ready, Set, Go! Free Marketing Resources

ALA: @ Your Library, http://www.ala.org/@yourlibrary

Users can access information about the @ Your Library Campaign, including recent news and participating libraries as well as detailed information about related campaigns. Logos in multiple languages can be downloaded, and a "Public Awareness Tools and Resources" section provides users with access to free PSAs (in both print and video formats) and a guide for *Marketing @ your library.*®

ALA Public Programs Office (PPO), http://www.ala.org/offices/ppo

The ALA PPO provides leadership, training, resources, and networking opportunities that can help librarians host cultural experiences for patrons. Their Programming Librarian initiative (http://www.programminglibrarian.org/home.html) provides planning tools and online learning opportunities. The ALA Cultural Communities Fund and other PPO programs are also highlighted on this site.

ALA Resources, http://www.ala.org/offices/

"Offices" are units of the ALA that address broad interests and issues of concern to ALA members and the general public. Examples are the Office for Diversity, the Office for Intellectual Freedom, and the Office for Literacy and Outreach.

Library Media and Public Relations (PR), http://www.ssdesign.com/librarypr/

This website contains a toolbox and articles relating to library marketing and PR. The "toolbox" feature contains free clip art, symbols, website banners, bookmarks, and links to other resources, including tips for public librarians who are designing websites. Current visitors to the website can view a podcast on publicity and PR for promoting a summer reading program at a library.

Market Your Library from Gale Cengage Learning, http://www.gale.cengage.com/InContext/collateral.htm

Gale Cengage Learning provides free downloadable marketing materials (in PDF format) for libraries and websites.

Marketing, http://www.libsuccess.org/index.php?title=Marketing

This site includes links to library marketing resources and ideas and makes them available at one convenient site. The content includes marketing success stories sample marketing plans, technology tips for social media, and gaming as an outreach tool.

The next chapter discusses using social media to market your library.

Chapter 4

Communication and Outreach with Social Media

Introduction

No discussion of marketing for libraries would be complete without a discussion of social media. In the last few years, we've seen a dramatic increase in the number of social networking websites and in the use of social media by all segments of the population. In fact, according to a 2013 study the Pew Internet Project, 73 percent of online adults use social media. (The report can be found at http://www.pewinternet.org/fact-sheets/social-network ing-fact-sheet/; it contains a great deal of useful information that can help you explore who might be a good target for your social media marketing.)

Popular social media sites currently include Facebook, Twitter, Instagram, and Pinterest. There is no way that one library can be actively involved in all of the social networking sites on the Internet; there are just too many and they are constantly changing. This chapter will help you decide which tools are right for your library's marketing efforts. We'll explore incorporating social media into your marketing plan, deciding which social media tool(s) to use to market your library, and managing your social media.

Planning to Use Social Media

When your library decides to start using social media, it is important to make sure that you have a plan. That plan should include:

- the social media websites you will use to market your library;
- what kind of content you will put online;
- who is going to monitor and update the social media websites; and
- how you will assess your success.

As you create your social media marketing plan, make sure that it fits into your larger marketing plan. For instance, you should think about what kind of message you want to send and who you want to target. Think about how the use of a social media tool is going to advance the goals of your larger marketing plan. Social media can be fun, but it can also take a lot of time from your staff. Make sure that you are intentional about your choices when incorporating social media into your marketing plan.

Choosing the Right Tool

When your library decides to start using social media, the first thing you have to determine is what tools you want to use. We recommend starting with just one or two social networking sites, because it can be hard to manage too many at once. You want to make sure that you follow through with your social media marketing plan and trying to manage too many sites can cause you to lose focus. Pick one or two sites that will be relatively easy for you to manage over an extended period of time.

There are plenty of free social media sites, so choosing the right ones for your library can sometimes seem overwhelming. It doesn't have to be too complicated, though. Just make sure that the tools you choose fit in with your larger marketing plan. Think about your needs and the type of message that you want to send. Do you want to share a lot of pictures? Try Instagram. Do you want to update often, with quick messages? Try Twitter. Table 4.1 will give you an idea of how some of the more popular social media websites can be used.

Another thing to consider when choosing the social media websites is your audience. What social media sites do your patrons use? It's possible that different groups of patrons are using different tools. For instance, teens might go to a different social media site (like Snapchat) than the ones their parents use (like Facebook). Take a look at your marketing plan and determine which audience you want to target. Then decide which tool is the best to use to reach that audience. If you're not sure which social media sites your patrons prefer, do a survey. Don't try to guess! Also, remember that sometimes social media sites wane in popularity. Check in with your patrons once in a while to make sure you're still where they are.

Social Media Website	URL	Potential Use
Facebook	http://www.facebook.com	A social networking site that allows users to post updates and share pictures and videos. Create a page for your library that your patrons can follow.
Flickr	http://www.flickr.com	A photo-sharing site. Upload pictures of events that have happened at your library or of popular or beautiful places in your town.
Instagram	http://instagram.com	Another photo-sharing site. Your patrons can follow your account and make comments on the photos that you upload. Be creative! Put photos of events at your library or of recent displays you have done. You could also do an Instagram campaign with images of your patrons (with their permission, of course)!
Pinterest	http://www.pinterest.com	An online curation tool. This website is a great way to create online displays. For instance, you might pin the covers of books that have recently been added to your collection.
Snapchat	http://www.snapchat.com	A service that allows users to send photos or videos via text. The images are removed 10 seconds after viewing. It is a popular social networking tool among teens and young adults.
Tumblr	http://www.tumblr.com	An online curation tool. This website is a great way to create online displays. For instance, you might pin the covers of books that have recently been added to your collection.
Twitter	http://twitter.com	A microblogging service that allows you to share brief (140 character) messages. Your patrons can follow your posts and you can follow—and retweet—their posts. Images and videos can also be uploaded to your Twitter account.
WordPress	http://wordpress.org	WordPress is a popular tool for making blogs and other kinds of websites. If you're hoping to create a blog to share some of the events happening in your library, WordPress is a useful tool. Some libraries have even used WordPress to create their library websites!
YouTube	http://www.youtube.com	A video-sharing tool. You could upload videos of presentations that have happened at your library. You could also do a YouTube contest and ask your patrons to make videos describing what they love about the library. That would be a lot of content for your YouTube channel and would be a great way to advertise all the things your library does for the community!

Managing Social Media

Once you have chosen the social media tool you will use, make sure that you have a plan to manage it. First, decide who will be responsible for updating and monitoring it.

Be clear about whose responsibility this is; outline clear expectations for how often your sites will be updated, when you will check for comments and responses, and what kind of content is appropriate to post. There are various models out there for assigning these responsibilities. For instance, some libraries ask the person on the reference desk to update or respond as appropriate. Other libraries may assign this task to only one person. Whatever model you choose, make sure that there is one person who is your social media point person.

This person will be especially valuable if you have more than one social media site. It is important that the messages from all your social media sites are consistent and work together to market your library. For instance, if you include your library's branding on one site, make sure you do so for all of your sites. If you have the option to choose custom colors or themes, make sure that these are consistent across all of your social media. Also, ensure that advertisements about events contain the same message on all of your sites. You don't want to have different times for an event listed, as this will only cause confusion for your patrons.

One of the most challenging parts about using social media is making sure that all of your sites are updated frequently. Setting up an account is easy, but keeping it updated can be difficult, especially over the long term. However, updates are the one thing that will keep your patrons returning to your site. If the site contains nothing new every time a patron checks in, you will find that people eventually just stop looking at it. Of course, the frequency of your updates also depends on the type of social networking tool that you're using. People don't expect a new blog post on a WordPress account as frequently as they expect a new tweet on Twitter, but blog posts must be longer than tweets. Evaluate the number of updates you should have in a week and make sure you post that often. This should be an important part of your social marketing plan.

If coming up with new content sounds difficult, don't worry: there are plenty of types of content that can keep your social media interesting. The obvious thing to share on social media is information about your library. By all means, share news about recent acquisitions, new databases, or upcoming programs. But don't stop there. Not all of your posts have to be directly related to the library. Here are some examples:

- Provide updates about events going on in your community. Your patrons will appreciate hearing about local events, even if they're not happening at your library. You could also highlight your patrons' accomplishments, like local honor roll students. Think of your social networking sites as not only marketing tools, but also as information-sharing tools.

- Have a "Trivia Thursday" post on Twitter every week, where you ask a question and see how many of your patrons answer correctly.

- Post a photograph on Instagram and ask your patrons to try to identify it. (This could be especially fun if you have some local history materials in your library!)

- Ask your librarians to provide recommendations for books they're read recently. A link back to the catalog record would help your patrons enjoy the same items.

- Use Pinterest to create an online display related to an awareness week or month. For instance, you could curate an online display about women authors during Women's History Month.

- Do a Facebook poll to gather information about what types of events your patrons would like to see at your library. This allows you to promote your library and to get information about the population.

Remember that photographs and videos are also great content for social media. When possible, look for opportunities to include multimedia in your social media accounts. A picture of a great turnout at one of your library's events can tell a lot about what the library does for the community. You might want to assign one library staff member the job of being the library photographer. As we all know, it can easy to forget to take pictures or videos when you're in the middle of running an event. If one person is assigned the task, you're more likely to have content you can share on your social media sties.

As you decide what content to share, remember that social media is social! Whenever possible, make sure that your content shows off your library's personality and work to make it interactive. In fact, your patrons can help to create some of the content for you. It is common practice to share the posts of others on many social networking sites. If one of your patrons posts something that might be interesting to your other patrons, go ahead and re-post or retweet it. (Just make sure that you give them proper credit!) It can be especially good to repost things when someone says something nice about the library. Also, hashtags have become an increasingly popular way of tagging information on social networking sites. Create a hashtag (like #mypubliclibrary) that patrons can use when posting things about your library, so that people will see it and connect it to you. Try to make the hashtag as specific and local as possible. For instance, you might ask your patrons to post images of the library or of things they've checked out at the library on Instagram and label them with your library's hashtag. You can also have patrons create content for you. For instance, you might ask patrons to create videos about your library that could be uploaded to your library's YouTube channel. A contest with a prize at the end is a great way to promote your library, your social marketing sites, and to get people talking about your library.

As you work with your social media, remember that it's not all about posting content, but is also about interacting with people. Many social networking sites allow users to post comments, so make sure that you check those comments on a very regular basis and respond quickly to questions, complaints, and compliments. (Keep in mind, however, that it is important to have a social media policy in place so that you can appropriately deal with posts that are inappropriate or offensive. More information about creating social media policies can be found at the end of this chapter.) Social media is a visible forum and you want to make sure that you always put your best foot forward. Think of it as an opportunity to have a conversation with your community. Patrons—and potential patrons—have a chance to interact with you and you'll have an opportunity to learn more about them.

One caveat: make sure that you always respect your patrons' privacy when posting on social media. Some people don't like their images to be posted on social media, so, whenever possible, be sure to ask permission before you post a picture of a patron at an event or at the library. Plenty of your patrons will be happy to appear in your social media, but just make sure that you respect their privacy when appropriate.

Evaluating Social Media Success

When your library is using social media, it is always a good idea to do a periodic check-in. Because working with social media can be time consuming, you want to make sure that the effort your library staff expends is worth it. Signs of success include:

- An increase in followers on your social media site
- An increase of comments on content that you have posted
- An increase of reposts or retweets
- Library patrons telling you that they heard about an event or learned about your library from your social media website

Because social media is ever-changing, be sure to occasionally review which social media sites are gaining in popularity. You don't want to lose followers on sites you already maintain by neglecting those sites, but you also don't want to be left behind as new technologies emerge. Be dynamic in your assessment of your social media campaign!

If your social media marketing isn't getting you the results you want, ask yourself these questions:

- Do our patrons know that we are on social media? Do they know how to find us? If not, do we need to market our social media?
- Are we using the same social networking sites our patrons use?
- Do we post frequently enough?
- Is the content we post interesting and engaging for our patrons?
- Do we respond to our patrons' comments and questions in a timely manner?

Resources

Social Media for Libraries

- *Competencies for Social Networking in Libraries*, Betha Gutsche: https://www.webjunction.org/documents/webjunction/Competencies_for_Social_Networking_in_Libraries.html
- *Getting Started in Social Media Workbook*, Allegheny County Library Association: http://www.webjunction.org/documents/pennsylvania/PAdocument32.html

- *Library Social Media Use Webinar*, OCLC WebJunction: https://www.webjunction.org/events/webjunction/Library_Social_Media_Use.html
- *LinkedIn: Social Media in Libraries*, OCLC WebJunction: http://www.linkedin.com/groups/Social-Media-in-Libraries-3774821/about
- *Social Media for Public Libraries: Basics & Beyond*, Elise C. Cole: http://www.slideshare.net/craighen/social-media-for-public-libraries-basics-and-beyond
- *Social Networking & Web 2.0 Documents*, OCLC WebJunction: https://www.webjunction.org/explore-topics/social-web/documents.html
- *Social Networking Literacy Competencies for Librarians: Exploring Considerations and Engaging Participation*, Joe Murphy and Heather Moulaison: http://www.ala.org/acrl/sites/ala.org.acrl/files/content/conferences/confsandpreconfs/national/seattle/papers/328.pdf
- *Using Electronic Media*, Everyday Advocacy (American Library Association): http://www.ala.org/everyday-advocacy/speak-out/electronic-media

Library Social Media Examples

- Charlotte Mecklenburg Public Library (Charlotte, North Carolina): http://www.cmlibrary.org/about_us/info.asp?id=29
- Denver Public Library (Denver, Colorado): http://denverlibrary.org/social
- Haverhill Public Library (Haverhill, Massachusetts): http://www.haverhillpl.org/social-media/
- New York Public Library (New York, New York): http://www.nypl.org/voices/connect-nypl
- Pima County Public Library (Tuscon, Arizona): https://www.library.pima.gov/contact/social.php

Social Media Policies

Writing a Social Media Policy:

- *Creating a Social Media Policy*, TechSoup: http://www.techsoup.org/support/articles-and-how-tos/creating-a-social-media-policy
- *Creating a Social Media Policy: What We Did, What We Learned*, Elizabeth Breed: http://www.infotoday.com/mls/mar13/Breed—Creating-a-Social-Media-Policy.shtml
- *The Nonprofit Social Media Policy Workbook*, Idealware: http://idealware.org/reports/nonprofit-social-media-policy-workbook

Sample Social Media Policies:

- Cleveland Public Library (Cleveland, Ohio): http://www.cpl.org/TheLibrary/UsingtheLibrary/PolicyontheUseofCPLsSocialMediaSites.aspx

- Gleason Public Library (Carlisle, Massachusetts): http://www.gleasonlibrary.org/social_media.htm
- Wood River Public Library (Wood River, Illinois): http://woodriverlibrary.org/about/social-media-policy/

Popular Social Networking Sites

Since social media is dynamic, with new sites frequently emerging and older sites losing popularity, it's important to be aware of the social networking tools currently used by your patrons. The following sites list some of the websites you can consult for information about popular social media:

- Mashable: Social Media: http://mashable.com/category/social-media/
- Popular Mechanics: http://www.popularmechanics.com/
- Social Media Today: http://socialmediatoday.com/
- Wired: http://www.wired.com/

Social Media Management Tools

If you feel that you need some external help to manage your library's social media presence, the following tools are available (for a fee):

- BlissControl: http://blisscontrol.com
- Buffer: http://bufferapp.com
- CrowdBooster: http://www.crowdbooster.com
- Hootsuite: http://hootsuite.com
- SocialBro: http://www.socialbro.com
- SocialFlow: http://www.socialflow.com
- SocialOomph: http://www.socialoomph.com
- SproutSocial: http://www.sproutsocial.com
- Tweepi: http://tweepi.com
- TweetDeck: http://tweetdeck.com

Library Examples on Pinterest:

- http://pinterest.com/msstatelibrary/
- http://pinterest.com/addisonlibrary/
- http://pinterest.com/nplibrary/
- http://pinterest.com/missoulalibrary/

- http://pinterest.com/mcplspins/
- http://pinterest.com/missmadyb/
- http://pinterest.com/sjcpls/
- http://pinterest.com/martincountylib/
- http://pinterest.com/ndsl
- http://pinterest.com/larmctylibrary/boards/
- http://pinterest.com/NDSL/boards/
- http://pinterest.com/mcplspins/

Libraries on Twitter Shared in Chat:
- https://twitter.com/JaxIL_PL
- https://twitter.com/KzooLibrary
- https://twitter.com/Crawford_PubLib
- https://twitter.com/bcls
- https://twitter.com/cutpl
- https://twitter.com/MeridianLibrary
- https://twitter.com/MesaLibrary
- https://twitter.com/StateLawLibrary
- https://twitter.com/pbclibrary
- http://twitter.com/RyeFRR
- https://twitter.com/accessfreely
- https://twitter.com/aclib
- http://twitter.com/ThinkACLD
- https://twitter.com/BoothLibrary
- https://twitter.com/madybee1
- https://twitter.com/zplinfo
- https://twitter.com/NDStateLibrary
- https://twitter.com/CCLDBookmobile

Chapter 5

Fund-Raising

An effective marketing plan includes information about how you will fund your program or service. To successfully fund your library marketing projects, you'll have to be able to effectively develop relationships with potential donors. This chapter focuses on some ways you can raise support for and promote the library in your community through the networking that is done by library staff and friends' groups. You can also raise funds for the library by developing grant proposals to state and federal agencies, foundations, and private donors.

Developing Relationships

People in your community should be reminded (or told) about the services and resources that are offered by the library. Librarians need to make the library and themselves known to the public, rather than waiting for people to come into the library. People are willing to contribute to causes that are important to them, and librarians must find ways to let people know what is happening in the library. You may not realize it, but you can develop many relationships when working in a library. Each contact has the potential to place the library in the public view and to increase support. Think of ways that the people you deal with on a daily basis could have an impact on the library.

The following relationships can provide opportunities for librarians to reach out beyond the library doors. Take some time to think of how these could benefit the library.

- Librarians and patrons
- Librarians and staff
- Librarians and the board of trustees
- Librarians and the media
- Librarians and funders
- Librarians and business leaders
- Librarians and nonusers
- Librarians and volunteers
- Librarians and friends' groups

All of these relationships can be used, in different ways, to raise funds for your library. As you develop your marketing plan, keep these relationships in mind. The relationships that you have developed can be utilized by calling upon the individuals to help fund your program when the need arises.

Local Funding

The potential to find funding for your project can be with the stakeholders in the local community, and you should be prepared to make contacts with each person who is encountered inside or outside of the library. Your library staff should be ready to give an "elevator speech" whenever the opportunity arises. As mentioned previously, an "elevator speech" is used when you have a brief opportunity to tell someone about the highlights of your project or organization—in the time it would take to reach your destination in an elevator. Many librarians are prepared with interesting facts about library programs or services that can be told quickly to someone while they are riding in an elevator, standing in line at the grocery store, or attending a social gathering. Having short "stories" ready to share with anyone you meet is a great way to spread the news about what the library is doing. You may miss great fund-raising opportunities if you stand silently during an *elevator ride*!

Take some time to select key points about your library and to ask your staff for ideas that you could share with others. Following are examples of talking points for elevator speeches:

- Last summer *XXX* children participated in the summer reading program and they read *XXX* books.
- We deliver *XXX* books to seniors in the nursing facility each week.
- The library is working with the hospital to give books to the families of each newborn, and we invite them to the baby lap-sit program in the library. Did you know that reading to babies increases the literacy rate of children?
- *XXX* cans of food were collected for the food bank during our campaign to return overdue books. Fines were canceled when the books were returned with a contribution of food.

In each of these exchanges the librarian should be ready to give out a business card with the name, address, phone number, and website of the library so the person can contact the library for more information. Also, be ready to tell about the exciting plans the library has for future projects. Get your new contacts interested in the library, and have specific projects ready for them to provide assistance.

Friends' Groups

Friends' groups are volunteers who can play major roles in promoting libraries to their communities and helping libraries to achieve their strategic goals. These groups are vital to public, school, and academic libraries in their efforts to increase visibility and assist in fund-raising. Fund-raising efforts sponsored by friends' groups include a wide variety of events:

Sales
- Books
- Bricks
- Calendars
- Cookbooks
- Library logo merchandise
- Restaurant days (10% of sales goes to the library)

Events
- Art auctions
- Book signings
- Galas
- High teas
- Murder mystery
- Photo contests (with winning photos depicted on library calendars that are sold to the public)
- Prepackaged food sales
- Raffles
- "Read-a-Thons"
- Silent auctions

American Library Association's (ALA's) United for Libraries provides a comprehensive resource for friends' groups, including valuable materials on how to engage in effective fund-raising efforts. Examples of the fund-raising efforts of groups are available at their website listed at the end of this chapter.

Grants

Librarians have a solid record of writing successful grant proposals to obtain funding for projects. The ability to locate appropriate funding sources and the skills needed to develop grant proposals are easy to learn, and funds are available from private donors, foundations, and the government. There are several suggested sources at the end of this chapter that list potential grant sources. The Foundation Center also noted at the end of the chapter has online tutorials to aid in all aspects of the grant-writing process.

State and Federal Funding

Public librarians should be aware of federal funds that are available through the Grants to States program using a population-based formula. Funding from the Library Services and Technology Act (LSTA) is provided to the state library administrative agencies to support library efforts to

- expand services for learning and access to information and educational resources in a variety of formats, in all types of libraries, for individuals of all ages;
- develop library services that provide all users access to information through local, state, regional, national, and international electronic networks;
- provide electronic and other linkages between and among all types of libraries;
- develop public and private partnerships with other agencies and community-based organizations;
- target library services to individuals of diverse geographic, cultural, and socioeconomic backgrounds, to individuals with disabilities, and to individuals with limited functional literacy or information skills; and
- target library and information services to persons having difficulty using a library and to underserved urban and rural communities, including children from families with incomes below the poverty line.

Information about LSTA grants and other federal and state awards is available on the website of each state library. You should develop a relationship with the appropriate representative from your state library to learn about the funding that is available to support projects for your library. Following is a list of websites for each state:

Alabama: http://www.apls.state.al.us

Alaska: http://library.state.ak.us

Arizona: http://www.azlibrary.gov/

Arkansas: http://www.asl.lib.ar.us

California: http://www.library.ca.gov

Colorado: http://www.cde.state.co.us/cdelib

Connecticut: http://www.ctstatelibrary.org/

Delaware: http://libraries.delaware.gov/

Florida: http://dlis.dos.state.fl.us/index.cfm

Georgia: http://www.georgialibraries.org

Hawaii: http://www.librarieshawaii.org/

Idaho: http://libraries.idaho.gov/

Illinois: http://www.cyberdriveillinois.com/departments/library/

Indiana: http://www.in.gov/library/

Iowa: http://www.statelibraryofiowa.org/

Kansas: http://www.kslib.info/

Kentucky: http://www.kdla.ky.gov

Louisiana: http://www.state.lib.la.us

Maine: http://www.maine.gov/msl/

Maryland: http://msa.maryland.gov/msa/mdmanual/01glance/html/library.html

Massachusetts: http://mblc.state.ma.us/

Michigan: https://www.michigan.gov/libraryofmichigan

Minnesota: http://education.state.mn.us/MDE/StuSuc/Lib/StateLibServ/

Mississippi: http://www.mlc.lib.ms.us

Missouri: http://www.sos.mo.gov/library

Montana: http://home.montanastatelibrary.org/

Nebraska: http://www.nlc.state.ne.us/

Nevada: http://nsla.nevadaculture.org/

New Hampshire: http://www.nh.gov/nhsl

New Jersey: http://www.njstatelib.org

New Mexico: http://www.nmstatelibrary.org/

New York: http://www.nysl.nysed.gov

North Carolina: http://statelibrary.ncdcr.gov/

North Dakota: http://ndsl.lib.state.nd.us

Ohio: https://library.ohio.gov/

Oklahoma: http://www.odl.state.ok.us

Oregon: http://oregon.gov/OSL

Pennsylvania: http://www.portal.state.pa.us/portal/server.pt/community/bureau_of_
state_library/

Rhode Island: http://www.olis.ri.gov/

South Carolina: http://www.statelibrary.sc.gov/

South Dakota: http://www.sdstatelibrary.com

Tennessee: http://www.tennessee.gov/tsla/

Texas: http://www.tsl.state.tx.us

Utah: http://heritage.utah.gov/library

Vermont: http://libraries.vermont.gov/

Virginia: http://www.lva.virginia.gov/

Washington: http://www.sos.wa.gov/library/

West Virginia: http://www.librarycommission.wv.gov/

Wisconsin: http://dpi.wi.gov/libraries

Wyoming: http://www-wsl.state.wy.us

Foundations

A foundation is a charitable organization created by individuals or institutions for the purpose of distributing funds to support specific areas of interest. The best source for libraries to identify charitable institutions is the publications of the Foundation Center.

The national Foundation Center is located in New York City, with branches located in several libraries in larger cities across the country. In addition, the Foundation Center supports "Cooperating Collections," which are housed in libraries, community foundations, and other nonprofit resource centers throughout the United States. These resource centers provide a core of Foundation Center publications and supplementary materials useful in the grant-seeking process. Each Foundation Center has access to all the resources of the main center in New York, so check to find the one that is closest to you. The Foundation Center has a subscription database, *The Foundation Directory Online*, which includes 80,000 grantmakers and 500,000 different grants. Accessing this database will allow you to identify potential foundations whose funding interests match those of your library project.

Corporate Funding, Corporate Foundations, and Local Businesses

Corporations often have a related foundation that is designed for philanthropic or charitable giving. It is important to identify corporations that have philanthropic interests that match the needs of your library. Again, you can identify corporations that have giving interests similar to those of your library project by consulting the Foundation Center.

Example: A library in an ethnically diverse community developed a marketing plan that celebrates the cultures of the various groups. The activities included an artist series that features lectures, an art show, and artists-in-residence. Through the Foundation Center the library identified Wachovia as a likely corporate sponsor. Wachovia's funding priorities (as identified on their website, located through the Foundation Center) focus on arts and culture, with primary goals to

- facilitate access to and participation in cultural experiences for persons with low to moderate income and
- ensure the availability of a broad array of artistic opportunities or venues that reflect the diversity of the community.

The library could develop a proposal to Wachovia that reflects the goals of the corporation and the needs of the library. The possibilities are limitless—all librarians need is the knowledge of where to search for potential funding!

A formal grant proposal is not always needed to obtain corporate funding. Often you may contact the organization by phone or e-mail to ask about corporate sponsorship for a library project or activity. Corporations and local businesses may partner with a library in several ways:

- through capital support:
    - funding to support the project;
- through in-kind contributions of
    - equipment or
    - supplies;
- through marketing and advertising support:
    - providing advertisements in return for placement of the corporate logo on materials;
- through employee involvement:
    - employee volunteers for projects; and
- through networking opportunities with business associates:
    - referrals to other organizations that can provide support.

Following are some examples:

- A local grocer might provide snacks for an after-school homework program in return for
    - acknowledgement in the library or library publications or
    - a sign in the store advertising: Proud Sponsor of Library After-School Program.

- A business will provide money or in-kind contributions for a program in return for
  - acknowledgment in the library or library publications or
  - a sign in the business establishment advertising: Proud Sponsor of Library Program.
- A library develops a sponsor Hall of Fame that is displayed in the library, in library publications, and on posters.

Private Donors and Benefactors

Contributions from individuals are common to libraries. Many public libraries were made possible through individual contributions of property and collections, and many are located in houses donated by citizens of the community. There are many examples of the ways in which private donors contribute to the growth of libraries.

Libraries can set up formal giving programs for the general public, and they may also establish relationships with individuals who have special collections or interests in supporting the library. Consider

- a benefactor program with established levels of giving;
- contributions to commemorate birthdays, special events, and memorials;
- bequests or planned giving; and
- a capital campaign for a specified project (furniture, technology, building, etc.).

There are many more ways in which your library could participate in fund-raising activities than you might think. Your creativity will help you expand your original list.

Putting It All Together

The material and examples provided here are intended to get you started increasing the visibility of your library. Remember that communication is the key to effective marketing. Make the most of each opportunity presented to you.

Resources

Identify Stakeholders

- American Library Association: http://www.ala.org/everyday-advocacy/engage

Elevator Speeches

- New Jersey State Library: http://marketing.njstatelib.org/blogs/2013/dec/13/the_art_of_the_elevator_pitch

- American Library Association: http://www.ala.org/everyday-advocacy/speak-out/elevator-speech

Friends' Groups

- United for Libraries: http://www.ala.org/united/
- Friends' Groups: http://www.ala.org/united/friends
- Ilovelibraries: http://www.ilovelibraries.org/ways-advocate-friend

Fund-raising Ideas

- The Libri Foundation: http://www.librifoundation.org/fund.html
- Library Foundation of Los Angeles: https://www.lfla.org/store/
- American Library Association:
  - http://www.ala.org/tools/atoz/fundraising/fundraising
  - http://www.ala.org/advocacy/advleg/frontlinefundraising
  - http://www.ala.org/tools/libfactsheets/alalibraryfactsheet24

Grants

- LSTA: http://www.ala.org/advocacy/advleg/federallegislation/lsta
- Foundation Center: http://www.foundationcenter.org
- Scholastic List of Available Grants: http://www.scholastic.com/librarians/programs/grants.htm
- Library Grants Center: http://www2.salempress.com/
- Mackin Grant Channel: http://www.mackin.com/Library/Grants.aspx
- OCLC Web Junction: http://www.webjunction.org/explore-topics/budget-funding.html

Donor Recognition Examples

- San Diego, California: http://betsykschulz.com/the-fallbrook-library-mural-the-process/
- Oceanside, California: https://www.ci.oceanside.ca.us/gov/lib/support/donors.asp
- Johns Creek, Georgia: http://www.oceefriends.org/p/donor-wall.html
- Farmington, Michigan: http://www.farmlib.org/library/mime.html

Professional Resources

- *ALA Library Fund-raising: Selected Annotated Bibliography*: http://www.ala.org/tools/libfactsheets/alalibraryfactsheet24
- Association of Fundraising Professionals: http://www.afpnet.org/

Planned Giving

- American Library Association: http://www.ala.org/advocacy/advleg/frontlinefund raising/legacy_
- Utica, New York: http://www.uticapubliclibrary.org/support-the-library/planned-giving/
- Flanders, New Jersey: http://www.mopl.org/drupal/node/57

Appendix A

Glossary

Prepared by Sara Gillespie Swanson

Action Plan   The "to do" list section of the marketing plan. It includes an outline of specific tasks and describes what will be done, when each task will begin or be completed, who will accomplish the tasks, and the resources assigned to the project. (Chapter 2)

Annual Report   A document used to highlight the success experienced at your library during the previous year. (Chapter 3)

Boilerplate   A standard—and brief—description of a library that can be used for a number of different purposes. It includes statistics about the library and explains the importance and relevance of the library, the collection, and the staff. It can be used in the executive summary of the marketing plan. (Chapter 2)

Elevator Speech   A quick introduction to your library (or a library initiative) that can be given during the length of an elevator ride. It should include highlights and relevant statistics. Some of the statements from an elevator speech can be used in the executive summary of the marketing plan. (Chapters 2, 5)

Environmental Scan   The process of examining the various factors that may have an impact on the library and the community. (Chapters 1, 2)

Executive Summary   An overview of everything that will be presented in the marketing plan. It can be used as an introduction to the marketing plan or as an overview of the marketing plan to be presented for funding or approval from another authority. It should be written after the rest of the marketing plan is written. (Chapter 2)

Focus Group   A useful way to collect information about patrons and potential patrons. Focus groups involve interviewing community members who are targets of your marketing plan. (Chapter 1)

Foundation   A charitable organization created by individuals or institutions for the purpose of distributing funds to support specific areas of interest. Librarians can identify charitable institutions in the publications of the Foundation Center. (Chapter 5)

Four Ps of Marketing   Product, price, promotion, and place. The four Ps make up the strategy portion of the marketing plan. (Chapter 2)

Friends of the Library   Volunteers who can play major roles in promoting libraries to their communities and helping libraries to achieve their strategic goals. (Chapter 5)

Grants   Funding for the library from private donors, foundations, and the government. (Chapter 5)

Marketing Plan   A plan to market your library's services. It should match the goals and objectives of your library's strategic plan. (Chapter 1, 2)

Media List   A list that identifies the newspaper, radio, and television reporters who will publicize information about your library. (Chapter 3)

Media Plan   A plan for how the library will work with the media to share information about library events. (Chapter 3)

Newsletter   An effective way for libraries to communicate with their community of users and nonusers. Their content includes upcoming or past events, new acquisitions, a list of donors, feature stories, and a calendar of events. (Chapter 3)

Nominal Group Technique (NGT)   A nonthreatening method used to collect response from each person in a group setting. In NGT, all participants share their ideas and there is a group discussion after all ideas have been generated. (Chapter 1)

Press Kit   A folder that contains marketing materials about a speaker or event being held in the library. It can be given to media outlets before the event so that they have background information about and photos of the person who will be speaking or the event that will be taking place. (Chapter 3)

Press Release   A concise document that includes relevant information about your library's new program or service. It should contain precise information with an interesting title that catches the interest of your media representative. (Chapter 3)

Public Service Announcement (PSA)   A short announcement that can be read on radio or television in 10-, 30-, or 60-second spots. (Chapter 3)

Social Media Marketing Plan   A plan for using social media to market and promote your library. This plan should fit into the larger marketing and/or strategic plans. (Chapter 4)

Social Media Policy   A policy for both employees and patrons regarding the use of social media in the library. This policy allows you to appropriately deal with posts that are inappropriate or offensive. (Chapter 4)

Strategic Plan   A plan for the library that includes goals and objectives that can be used to plan for programs and services, collection development, budget justification, and marketing and public relations. (Chapter 1)

SWOT Analysis   A tool used to assess the internal and external factors affecting the environment. The strengths, weaknesses, opportunities, and threats are analyzed in a SWOT analysis. (Chapter 1)

Appendix B

Boilerplate Example

Prepared by Sara Gillespie Swanson

Located in Anytown, Anystate, the Anytown Public Library serves a population of 20,000 with a collection of 200,000 items including books, magazines, and media. Our staff serves our citizens from 12:00 P.M. to 8:00 P.M. on weekdays and from 12:00 P.M. to 6:00 P.M. on Saturdays and Sundays. With an annual circulation of 200,000, representing 100 items per capita, our specialized collections serve approximately 1,000 non-English speakers with four language materials, Chinese, Japanese, Spanish, and Vietnamese. We offer access to ten major databases and access to 24/7 reference service.

Story times are offered for lap-sits and preschoolers, and our children's department provides an exciting summer reading program for 1,000 children each summer. Our after-school programs serve 8,000 students in grades 4 to 12. Contact Mary Jones at 111–222–3333 or mjones@anytown.org.

Appendix C

Nominal Group Technique

Prepared by Sue Alman

The Friends of the Library decided to participate in a nominal group technique (NGT) exercise in preparation for determining the type of fund-raising project that would appeal to a broad audience. The director sent this notice to each of the 10 members of the Friends of the Library:

> On Friday morning we will meet together from 9 to 11 A.M. in the conference room to identify potential fund-raising options. Please bring a list of all the fund-raising ideas that you have received from library patrons or that you think would be interesting to people in our community who are loyal patrons and to those who have not used the library.
>
> Coffee and bagels will be available beginning at 8:45 A.M.

Step 1: Identify the facilitator prior to the announcement of the date. This can be anyone who knows the NGT process and can keep the group on target. Gather materials the day before the NGT session: flipcharts, Post-It™ notes or index cards, and tape.

Step 2: By 8:30 A.M. have room set up with coffee and bagels, materials, and seating for everyone.

Step 3: At 9:00 A.M., the facilitator should ask the participants to take their seats and explain that they are going to take part in a process to determine the best fund-raising projects for the library.

Step 4: The facilitator gives everyone a paper that repeats the purpose of the process—to identify potential fund-raising options—and asks the participants to write their ideas on the paper:

- **Round 1:** The facilitator asks each person to share one idea that will be written on the flipchart so that everyone can see it. There will be *no* discussion allowed—only the generation of ideas.

- **Round 2:** Same as round 1. A person may "pass" if he or she does not have an idea, and the facilitator will move on to the next person.

- **Round 3:** Same as round 1; however, each person is asked even if he or she "passed" in the previous round because he or she may have thought of an idea.

Each person shares one idea per round. The facilitator writes each idea on the flipchart and numbers it in consecutive order. The rounds are continued until all of the ideas have been generated.

Example:

The Friends of the Library who are participating in the nominal group technique are:

Bud	Sarah	Doris
John	Tom	Carolyn
Theresa	Ron	Marcy
Chris		

In *round 1* the following suggestions are made:

Bud: book sale

John: art auction

Theresa: photo contest (with winning photos depicted on library calendars to be sold to the public)

Chris: high tea

Sarah: gala

Tom: banquet

Ron: book signing

Doris: theatrical production

Carolyn: Chinese/silent auction

Marcy: Prepackaged food sales

In *round 2* the following suggestions are made:

Bud: restaurant "library night" (10% of sales goes to the library)

John: "pass"

Theresa: selling bricks

Chris: kiddie carnival

Sarah: cookbook sales

Tom: "pass"

Ron: booth or raffle at a larger event

Doris: bell ringers on street corners

Carolyn: gala

Marcy: "Poor Man's Dinner"

In *round 3* the following suggestions are made:

Bud: "pass"

John: wine and cheese event

Theresa: dessert party

Chris: selling gear with library logo

Sarah: "pass"

Tom: "pass"

Ron: paid services or events

Doris: flea market booth

Carolyn: "pass"

Marcy: "pass"

In *round 4* the following suggestions are made:

Bud: bingo/poker night with buy-in

John: "pass"

Theresa: "Read-a-Thons"

Chris: "pass"

Sarah: "pass"

Tom: "pass"

Ron: "pass"

Doris: "pass"

Carolyn: "pass"

Marcy: "pass"

In *round 5* no one has any suggestions.

The facilitator writes each idea on the flipchart, which looks like this:

1. book sale

2. art auction

3. photo contest (with winning photos depicted on library calendars that are sold to the public)

4. high tea

5. gala

6. book signing

7. theatrical production

8. Chinese/silent auction

9. prepackaged food sales

10. restaurant "library night" (10% of sales goes to the library)

11. selling bricks

12. kiddie carnival

13. cookbook sales

14. booth or raffle at a larger event

15. bell ringers on street corners

16. gala

17. "Poor Man's Dinner"

18. wine and cheese event

19. dessert party

20. selling gear w/library logo

21. paid services or events

22. flea market booth

23. bingo/poker night with buy-in

24. "Read-a-Thons"

Step 5: Each idea is reviewed and explained by someone who did *not* make the original suggestion. The idea may be discussed openly after it has been explained to the satisfaction of the person who suggested it.

Example:

- It is pointed out that the suggestion to have a "gala" (numbers 5 and 16) was listed two times, so number 16 is removed from the list.

- The group discusses the similarity between number 14 (booth or raffle) and number 22 (flea market booth) but decides to keep the ideas separate rather than combining them.

- The group decides that the silent auction could be held at any event, but they would vote separately for it.

Step 6:

- Each individual selects the five suggestions that he or she likes best and writes the suggestion on either an index card or a Post-It™ note.
- The individual ranks the five suggestions and places the ranked order on the card, 5 being the highest number of "points" and 1 being the lowest number of "points."
- The anonymous ballots are either "stuck" beside the corresponding idea on the flipchart or board or the index cards are collected and tallied.
- Those suggestions with the highest scores are then acted upon by the group or submitted to another group for further action.

Example:

Each person "sticks" his or her five ballots beside the corresponding idea on the flipchart. This provides a visual representation of the anonymous voting so that no one can say justifiably that his or her suggestion wasn't selected even though "everyone was in favor of it!" The results listed below indicate the number of people (votes) who select each of the suggestions and the sum of the points that they awarded. The suggestions that receive the largest number of votes and the highest number of points narrow the original list from 24 to 8. The group can then focus on how to plan for these events. Their decision could result in another NGT or general discussion, or these results could be submitted to another planning group. (Top votes are in boldface type.)

1. **book sale (5 votes/20 points)**
2. art auction (2 votes/6 points)
3. photo contest (with winning photos depicted on library calendars that are sold to the public)
4. high tea (1 vote/1 point)
5. **gala (9 votes/40 points)**
6. **book signing (8 votes/38 points)**
7. theatrical production
8. **Chinese/silent auction (10 votes/43 points)**
9. prepackaged food sales (1 vote/2 points)
10. **restaurant "library night" (10% of sales goes to the library) (8 votes/25 points)**
11. selling bricks (1 vote/2 points)
12. kiddie carnival (2 votes/6 points)

13. cookbook sales (2 votes/8 points)

14. **booth or raffle at a larger event (9 votes/17 points)**

15. bell ringers on street corners

16. Gala

17. "Poor Man's Dinner" (1 vote/3 points)

18. **wine and cheese event (6 votes/21 points)**

19. dessert party (2 votes/5 points)

20. selling gear w/library logo (3 votes/3 points)

21. paid services or events (2 votes/7 points)

22. flea market booth (4 votes/8 points)

23. bingo/poker night with buy-in (1 vote/5 points)

24. **"Read-a-Thons" (8 votes/25 points)**

Appendix D

John Cotton Dana Library Public Relations Awards

John Cotton Dana Awards

The John Cotton Dana competition, sponsored in conjunction with the H.W. Wilson Foundation, the American Library Association and EBSCO, is held annually, and awards are made to those libraries that have submitted exemplary public relations plans. The public relations materials developed by several libraries that received John Cotton Dana Awards are listed in this appendix.

CEDAR RAPIDS PUBLIC LIBRARY REBRANDING CAMPAIGN 2011

Application for the

JOHN COTTON DANA LIBRARY PUBLIC RELATIONS AWARD

for the consideration of

THE JOHN COTTON DANA AWARD COMMITTEE

Figure 1. Reprinted with permission from Amber Mussman and Katie Geiken

Summary

In the wake of a devastating flood, the Cedar Rapids Public Library is taking advantage of an unprecedented opportunity to reimagine library service and enhance the Library's impact as an advocate for literacy and lifelong learning. During this pivotal time, the 2011 Cedar Rapids Public Library Rebranding Campaign invited Cedar Rapidians to broaden their expectations of a great library and recognize the tremendous library experience available today. This nine-month rebranding initiative has heightened awareness of the Library as the entire community looks forward to the rebuilding and opening of the new main facility downtown in the summer of 2013.

Narrative

Introduction:

The Cedar Rapids Public Library (CRPL) was destroyed in a devastating flood in June of 2008. Over 160,000 books and other materials were lost and the library building itself was determined by the Federal Emergency Management Agency to be a total loss. Construction is underway on a new library, which will open in summer 2013.

While society changes and technology evolves, the mission of the CRPL—to be a passionate advocate for literacy and lifelong learning—remains timeless. The CRPL serves over 125,000 citizens and welcomed more than 500,000 visitors to its temporary main location in 2011. Circulation continues to increase each year, reaching over 800,000 items in 2011.

Needs assessment:

As the CRPL began to build a state-of-the-art downtown library, Library staff recognized an opportunity to review the effectiveness of the Library brand in the community and reinvent the brand to match the community's excitement for the new Library. Prior to this rebranding project, the Library brand was inconsistent and difficult to use. When questioned, community members could not distinguish between the CRPL brand and those of libraries in neighboring communities. A goal of the rebranding project was to help Cedar Rapidians associate the word "library" with their own Cedar Rapids Public Library.

Additionally, connotations associated with the word "library" were limiting the expectations of community members. Most people have strong, usually positive associations with libraries, often involving childhood memories of library visits. With the groundbreaking design of the new facility and the evolving role of the CRPL as an innovative community center, a goal of the new brand was to help the CRPL exceed expectations by creating and maintaining a buzz around all library events.

Planning:

Library Public Information Officer Amber Mussman assembled and led a design team consisting of Library Director Bob Pasicznyuk; Library Design and Marketing Specialist Amy Ackman; and professionals from OPN Architects and deNovo Alternative Marketing. The following are goals, tactics and desired attributes that resulted from the design team's planning process:

I. Goal: Develop a library brand that would complement the design and idea of the new main Library.

   A. Planning Tactic: Hire deNovo Alternative Marketing to maximize impact of the rebranding efforts.

   B. Planning Tactic: Incorporate new Library project leaders into discussions from the beginning so that the rebranding team understands the design concepts that inspired the building's design.

   Desired Campaign Attributes:

   1. Includes a new CRPL logo that will match the color scheme while reflecting the innovative nature of the new facility.

   2. Capitalizes on growing media coverage of the new Library by celebrating current Library programs and what it will offer when the permanent main library opens downtown.

II. Goal: Align brand concept with the mission of the Cedar Rapids Public Library.

   A. Planning Tactic: Conduct focus groups with Library staff to gain their perspective of customer sentiment toward the CRPL; identify perceived competitors; and understand the attributes that distinguish the CRPL from competitors.

   B. Planning Tactic: Conduct focus groups with the public to identify words and feelings associated with the Library, and understand the public's thoughts on the future of the CRPL.

   Desired Campaign Attributes:

   1. Emphasizes and celebrates the Library's unique attributes and achievements.

   2. Anticipates competition from neighboring libraries, online search engines, storefront and online book retailers, and all venues aiming to earn the free time of Cedar Rapidians so that the CRPL can remain relevant and become a top-of-mind research, entertainment, and educational choice.

   3. Creates a personal, emotional connection to the Library's mission and work.

III. Goal: Gain new advocates and increase awareness of the Library through brand recognition.

   A. Planning Tactic: Identify target audiences for the branding campaign.

   B. Planning Tactic: Recognize staff members as the Library's strongest brand ambassadors and involve them in all phases of brand development.

From *Crash Course in Marketing for Libraries: Second Edition* by Susan W. Alman and Sara Gillespie Swanson. Santa Barbara, CA: Libraries Unlimited. Copyright © 2015.

C. Planning Tactic: Consider feedback from focus groups in all phases of implementation.

<u>Desired Campaign Attributes:</u>

1. Strengthens the Library's ability to advocate effectively by targeting the following audiences—Library staff, current patrons, community members, City Council.

2. Entices broader audiences to take advantage of Library services, programs and resources.

Implementation Tactics and 2011 Timeline of Creative Activity:

With desired campaign attributes in mind, the Library developed and executed an activity plan based on the following implementation tactics:

- Work with a design team to develop a new logo and brand standards
- Establish a campaign to excite the community about the Library
- Execute the new brand standards throughout the Library and all touch points

January through March—Logo Creation: The logo, created by the design team, is influenced by the architecture of the new Library and emphasizes the word LIBRARY. The parentheses-like graphics denote that which is contained within the new building while complementing the red ellipse which is a focal point within and on top of the building. The green color reflects the forward thinking design of the Library, and its commitment to sustainability.

The parentheses-like graphics also highlight the letters "ARY," a suffix that can be used in a variety of ways to tie the Library to multiple subjects in the community and in the Library itself. For example: In the Library, cookbooks may be emphasized by a section with the word: CulinARY—using the parentheses-like graphics and "ARY" pulled from the logo.

April—Brand Standards: In order to keep branding consistent across all platforms, the design team created standards after the logo was completed. These standards include specified fonts, colors, sizes and regulations on use of the logo.

May—Internal Launch: The Library Director supported the design team's introduction of the brand to the Library staff at a special meeting. The presentation explained how staff feedback and the information gathered from focus groups were incorporated into the brand development process. Each staff member received a new, logo-emblazed name tag, lanyard, and water bottle. The staff also was among the first to view and provide feedback on a video designed to be part of the public launch.

June–August—Public Launch and ARY Campaign: The public campaign featured a number of creative uses of the "ARY" suffix from the Library logo to tease the new logo and launch the new brand. Campaign components included:

Billboards: A series of rotating electronic billboards in a high traffic area ran during the week leading up to the launch date. These billboards were white with "ARY" words mimicking the logo's style—imaginary, extraordinary, literary—and the date of the launch on the bottom. On the date of the launch, the billboards switched to the new library logo.

Website: In order to provide the best service to customers in the virtual realm, the CRPL worked with a local web firm to build a new website to be launched simultaneously with the public launch of the brand. The "virtual branch" included all new brand standards and greatly improved ease of use and design. A mobile site also was deployed, granting uncomplicated, mobile access to the most frequented areas of the website, as well as information on Library locations and hours.

Video: Complementing the website launch, the Library shared a video showing the "ARY" words and new logo on YouTube, Facebook and Twitter. This animated short was a fun way to get the public to relate to the campaign and create excitement about the Library.

Farmers' Market: The day before the logo launch, volunteers spent a Friday night "tagging" downtown sidewalks and streets (using spray chalk and with city permission) with a variety of "ARY" words, along with the Library's website address. The next morning during one of the city's popular Farmers' Markets more than 17,000 people walked the streets of downtown, crossing over these chalk tags, stopping to comment and take pictures. Library staff and volunteers invited the public to become part of the branding campaign by having their picture taken with their own "ARY" word. The images were then shared through social networks and tagged pictures spread the message further.

Signature Event: The campaign culminated on September 9 with an event called "Inside Out with Alton Brown." The evening, which featured celebrity chef and unconventional author Alton Brown, was designed to raise awareness of the Library and challenge assumptions. This inaugural Inside Out event was announced on August 9 and funds raised though ticket sales supported the new library project.

The event sold out quickly. The audience included regular Library patrons and many new people who do not typically attend Library programs. Attendees traveled from all over the city, county, and state to do something unexpected. This successful event embodied the concepts behind the new library brand from start to finish and also provided an additional venue at which to celebrate the "ARY" campaign.

From *Crash Course in Marketing for Libraries: Second Edition* by Susan W. Alman and Sara Gillespie Swanson. Santa Barbara, CA: Libraries Unlimited. Copyright © 2015.

Evaluation

I. Goal: Develop a library brand that would complement the design and idea of the new main Library.

- Developed and launched brand across all platforms in August 2011.

- Launched a new CRPL website and held a sold out signature event, both featuring the new brand and its connection to the new main library.

II. Goal: Align brand concept with the mission of the Cedar Rapids Public Library.

- The 59 members of the CRPL staff were involved throughout the branding process, becoming effective brand ambassadors. They connected directly with the more than 70,000 Library visitors in August and September 2011.

- More than 17,000 community members became part of the ARY campaign at the Farmers' Market in August 2011, stopping by the Library booth for a picture or responding to the chalk "tags" throughout the streets downtown.

- The signature event Inside Out with Alton Brown was unconventional and entertaining, reminding the audience that cookbooks and fun can be borrowed from the Library on a daily basis.

III. Goal: Gain new advocates and increases awareness of the Library through brand recognition.

- The CRPL saw a 36% increase in library cards issued in August 2011 over August 2010.

- Unique visitors to the website increased by 44% in the five months following the campaign.

- The amount of time spent by each visitor on the website increased by 33% in the same time period. The number of pages viewed increased by 19%.

- Throughout the public launch, the CRPL saw a 362% increase in "Likes" on Facebook.

- From August through December 2011, the CRPL circulated 349,909 items (a 12% increase over the same five month period of the prior year).

- From August through December 2011, 10,539 people attended CRPL programs, both on and off-site. This is an increase in program participation of 54% over the same time period of the prior year.

- The Inside Out event allowed the CRPL to celebrate plans to build an unexpected Library with a sold out crowd of 550 at an unexpected Library event.

Conclusion

As a municipal library, the CRPL's main source of annual revenue is the City of Cedar Rapids' allocation of local tax dollars from residents. From an advocacy standpoint, it is crucial for citizens to recognize that the CRPL is creating a valuable product with their tax dollars. The new brand continues to bring the value of the Cedar Rapids Public Library to life in Cedar Rapids as we build back stronger and share our story.

CEDAR RAPIDS PUBLIC LIBRARY REBRANDING CAMPAIGN 2011

SUPPORTING MATERIALS

Video

A video was made to introduce the public to the new logo and the campaign. See the video at: http://connect.crlibrary.org/2012/03/02/cedar-rapids-public-library/

.

Info Cards

These business card size info cards are perfect for quick reference of library locations and hours. A QR code leads to the Library website.

Business Cards

Business cards for staff include the new Library branding, as well as a QR code which leads to the individual's email. The back side includes basic Library information.

Letterhead

The new letterhead design carries the Library branding, using the curving colors along the bottom.

Note Cards

Library note cards are simple and perfect for any occasion.

New Patron Information

We transformed a former tri-fold brochure into a 2.5" by 8.5" bookmark that includes basic library information for new cardholders. It can be folded in thirds to fit perfectly into a wallet or pocket for easy reference.

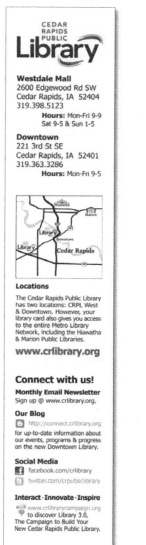

CEDAR RAPIDS PUBLIC Library

Westdale Mall
2600 Edgewood Rd SW
Cedar Rapids, IA 52404
319.398.5123
Hours: Mon-Fri 9-9
Sat 9-5 & Sun 1-5

Downtown
221 3rd St SE
Cedar Rapids, IA 52401
319.363.3286
Hours: Mon-Fri 9-5

Locations
The Cedar Rapids Public Library has two locations: CRPL West & Downtown. However, your library card also gives you access to the entire Metro Library Network, including the Hiawatha & Marion Public Libraries.

www.crlibrary.org

Connect with us!
Monthly Email Newsletter
Sign up @ www.crlibrary.org.

Our Blog
http://connect.crlibrary.org
for up-to-date information about our events, programs & progress on the new Downtown Library.

Social Media
facebook.com/crlibrary
twitter.com/crpubliclibrary

Interact · Innovate · Inspire
www.crlibrarycampaign.org
to discover Library 3.0,
The Campaign to Build Your
New Cedar Rapids Public Library.

The Benefits
Technology Center
Fax, copy & print your documents, take a free computer class, and enjoy free access to our computers & wireless service.

QuickFlicks
Reserve & borrow the latest dvds & video games at http://quickflicks.crlibrary.org.

Online Databases
Access over 25 online databases & indexes from our website.

Downloadable eBooks & Audiobooks
Check out our selection at http://mln.lib.overdrive.com.

Downloadable Music
Cedar Rapids residents can download 3 free music tracks each week on Freegal via our website.

Programming for all ages
Attend story time, music events, arts & crafts programs, book discussions, author visits, community collaborations & more! See our complete calendar of events at www.crlibrary.org.

Interlibrary Loan
If we don't have what you're looking for, we can probably get it for you! Interlibrary loan is available for a nominal fee.

The Basics
Loan periods
7 days- DVDs & video games
10 days- Quick Picks & magazines
21 days- Books, audio books & CDs

Returns
All items (except QuickFlicks) may be returned to 24-hr. drops at
CRPL West & Downtown
Marion Public Library
Hiawatha Public Library
Any metro Hy-Vee grocery store

Renewals
Two renewals are allowed for most items. Renew anytime online or call our self-serve line 319.398.7405.

Fines
$.20 per day, per children's item
$.25 per day, per adult item
$1 per day for video games
If fines exceed $20, library privileges will be suspended.

Lost or stolen library cards
Report lost or stolen cards immediately to avoid being responsible for unauthorized use.

Lost or damaged items
Charges for lost or damaged items will be assessed to cardholder's account.

Want More?
Additional information available at
www.crlibrary.org

Library Signs

All signage within the Library itself was redone to reflect the new brand standards.

CEDAR
RAPIDS
PUBLIC
Library

Hours

MONDAY–FRIDAY
9 am- 9 pm

SATURDAY
9 am- 5 pm

SUNDAY
1 am- 5 pm

www.crlibrary.org

www.crlibrary.org

A newly designed website launched with the rebranding campaign in August. The site is much more user friendly and the design follows the new style requirements.

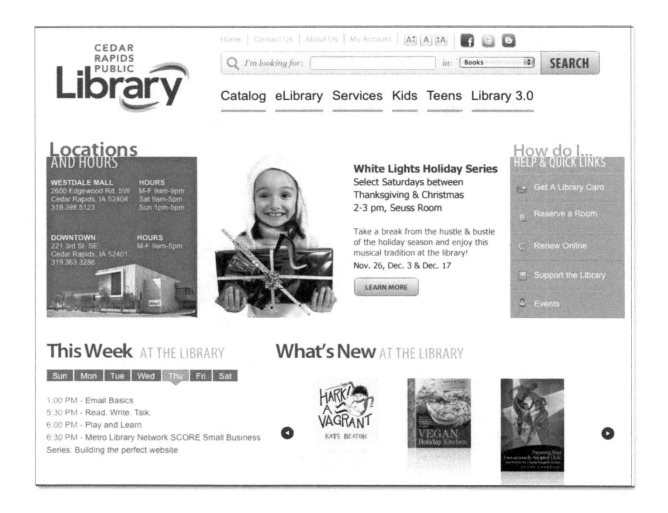

Operational Report

A revamped Operational Report is included in the Board of Trustees meeting packet each month. It includes valuable statistics and charts to make it an easy read for Trustees and the public.

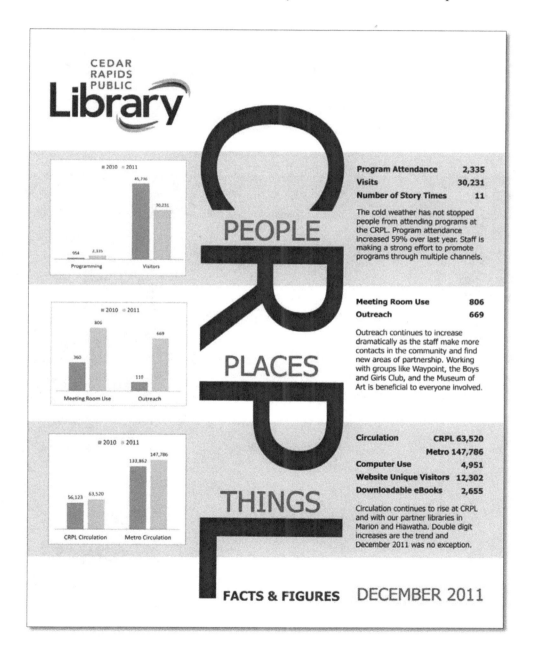

From *Crash Course in Marketing for Libraries: Second Edition* by Susan W. Alman and Sara Gillespie Swanson. Santa Barbara, CA: Libraries Unlimited. Copyright © 2015.

e-Newsletter

The electronic monthly newsletter was redesigned to take the brand directly to the more than 12,000 subscribers.

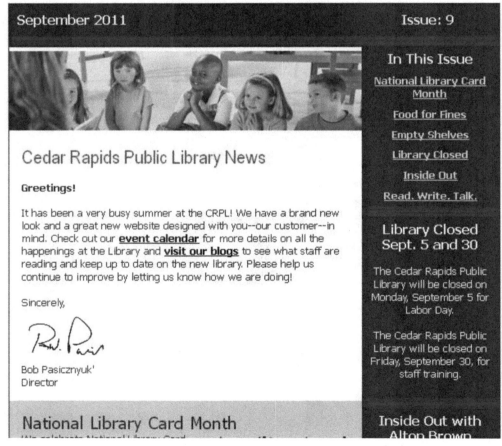

Billboards

A series of billboards rotated for a week leading up to the launch of the new logo.

Tagging

A group of volunteers led by Library PIO Amber Mussman used spray chalk to "tag" the ARY and chalked in a variety of words throughout downtown Cedar Rapids.

Farmers' Market

More than 17,000 citizens crossed over more than a dozen "tags" at the Farmers' Market held the following morning.

Farmers' Market

People were invited to have their picture taken with their very own "ARY" word. We had a list of words available and more than 40 people or families participated. Dozens more stopped to chat about the campaign. Pictures were uploaded to Facebook and people tagged themselves, spreading the message even further.

From *Crash Course in Marketing for Libraries: Second Edition* by Susan W. Alman and Sara Gillespie Swanson. Santa Barbara, CA: Libraries Unlimited. Copyright © 2015.

ARY Poster

The images were carried over into marketing materials and used throughout the year. This poster is used regularly on our digital signage within the Library.

Stickers

Stickers were given out at the Farmers' Market and the Library throughout the campaign.

Facebook

Using the images from the Farmers' Market we were able to create a new Facebook welcome page and banner image.

Name Tags

Staff received new nametags and lanyards. Programming staff received polo shirts to wear while running Library programs. Library staff was invited to purchase polo shirts and can wear them at work without the lanyard.

Rebranding In the News

The Library is the focus of newspaper articles celebrating the launch of the new website and logo. Cedar Rapids Gazette 8/5/2011

Photo: Cedar Rapids Public Library

A night view of the planned $49 million, 94,000 square-foot Cedar Rapids Public Library which is to be built in the 400 block of Fourth Ave. SE. The block is currently occupied by True North Companies Inc.

The opening of a new Cedar Rapids Public Library might be a couple of years out, but the excitement is starting now with the launch later this month of a new website and logo designed to resemble the future facility's unique architecture.

Cedar Rapids library to launch new logo, website

Initiative to launch Aug. 19

"We wanted to create a brand and a logo that reflect a more modern library and relate to the building itself," said library spokeswoman Amber Mussman.

As for the new website — which will debut along with the new logo on Aug. 19 — officials hope it will become a virtual library branch. With user-friendly portals allowing patrons to check out electronic materials, browse the stock and hold books, the new site will provide a glimpse into the upgrades and convenience of the future library, Mussman said.

The new facility, which will cost $49 million to build, stock and staff, is scheduled to open in summer 2013 across Fourth Avenue SE from Greene Square Park. Since the 2008 flood washed out the library's former space on First Street SE, it has been operating out of branches in the Westdale Mall and on Third Street SE in downtown.

Mussman said the temporary accommodations, while not a feasible long-term solution, have taught library officials more about the community's needs, and the library is committed to maintaining its Westdale branch even after the new downtown location opens.

"We are investing carefully in that space because it has been so great," she said.

In light of all the changes to the library system, Mussman said, a team of library staffers began working months ago to develop a new and improved brand and logo for the Cedar Rapids Public Library. The end result is an image that officials hope will get people thinking about the new, state-of-the-art facility.

"Our new logo is really representative of the energy and movement that the new building will have," Mussman said. "It will be less reflective of the materials and more reflective of the building's architecture, which will stand the test of time."

Buy this photo

The Cedar Rapids Public Library will officially unveil this new logo on Aug. 19, 2011, along with a new website that officials hope will become a virtual library branch. (Cedar Rapids Public Library)

The logo is accented by ellipses, which are a trademark in the new library's architectural designs. The logo colors are red, dark gray and a "modern" green, hinting at the facility's efforts to be environmentally friendly.

The new website, which Mussman said "will be dramatically different," will go live with the logo debut later this month. Among its new features is one enabling patrons to check the library's available materials before popping into one of the locations. The new site also will simplify a program allowing readers to check out e-books, music and other materials on line.

"It's going to be beautiful," she said.

The new site grew out of a realization that more people are using the library these days without leaving their homes.

"We wanted to create more of a virtual branch, and this is our first step toward doing that," she said.

Ange Gillis, 40, of Cedar Rapids, said she already visits crlibrary.org frequently and is thrilled at the idea of an updated library web presence.

"I already use the current website quite a bit to see what they have and put holds on books," Gillis said Friday while browsing the audio book section in the library's Westdale Mall branch. "So if they could expand it, that would be great."

"Inside Out"

Alton Brown appeared as the inaugural celebrity for "Inside Out", a new speaker series to support the Library. Included are two articles published about this extremely successful CulinARY event.

"Inside Out" In the News

Focus on Foundation

Library turns itself Inside Out to reach new audiences

As the Cedar Rapids Public Library continues planning for a marvelous new downtown facility, it is reaching out in new ways to remind the community that the library is a source of enrichment and learning for all.

This fall the library launched an innovative annual speaker series called Inside Out – sponsored by the Foundation and designed to take the library to the community through an evening of events surrounding an appearance by an unconventional author. The Inside Out series strives to introduce the community to remarkable authors, attract a varied audience, partner with other valued community organizations, and increase awareness and support for the library.

The inaugural Inside Out event held September 9 with bestselling author and celebrity chef Alton Brown raised more than $22,000 for the Library 3.0 Campaign.

Brown, who is the author of six best-selling books, host of Food Network's "Good Eats" and commentator on "Iron Chef America" spoke to a sold-out crowd of 550 people at Theatre Cedar Rapids. A pre-show cocktail reception for 75 was held prior to the event for an additional fee.

Inside Out with Alton Brown fulfilled another objective of the new speaker program – community collaboration – by promoting awareness of local organizations that provide food assistance to people in need. A "Food for Fines" campaign at the Cedar Rapids, Marion and Hiawatha Public Libraries encouraged patrons to bring nonperishable food items to the libraries, with each donated can or package exchanged for a $1 reduction in library fines. "Food for Fines" raised more than 2500 pounds of food which was donated to the HACAP Food Reservoir.

Future Inside Out speaker events will be designed to attract other audiences while building the library's reputation as a place that creates exciting events and provides adventures in learning for people of all ages and interests.

Award-winning chef and best-selling author Alton Brown shows his support for the Cedar Rapids Public Library.

The Cedar Rapids Public Library hosts a sold-out crowd of 550 at Theatre Cedar Rapids for the Inside Out with Alton Brown event on September 9, 2011.

The inaugural Inside Out event held September 9 with bestselling author and celebrity chef Alton Brown raised more than $22,000 for the Library 3.0 Campaign.

SATURDAY, SEPTEMBER 10, 2011 The Gazette 3A

Fun with food

Alton Brown keeps TCR audience in stitches

By Angie Holmes
The Gazette

CEDAR RAPIDS — Ignoring the flickering lights indicating the main event was about to start, Food Network star Alton Brown continued to sign autographs and pose for pictures at a reception before his lecture last night at Theatre Cedar Rapids.

The Cedar Rapids Public Library presented its first "Inside Out" performance to a sold-out audience. The performance, as well as the preshow reception, benefited the library, which will be rebuilt after being destroyed in the Floods of 2008.

"I've got a soft spot for libraries," Brown said.

But then he admitted his real motivation for fitting the Cedar Rapids show into his busy schedule.

"I have a bucket list," he said. "And on it was to visit the birthplace of Ashton Kutcher."

Before his lecture, "10 Things I'm Pretty Sure I'm Sure About Food," he presented a box of books he is donating to the new Cedar Rapids Public Library.

Sitting on edge of the stage, he went through the box and explained the books. The collection included his own books, including "I'm Just Here for the Food" and "Good Eats."

Other books suited for Iowans were "The Story of Corn" and the "Food Substitutions Bible" — because Iowa is "prone to natural disasters."

He explained his lectures change each time he gives them. Last night's lecture was no exception as each point he made was interspersed with personal stories and questions from the audience.

His lecture was a frank discussion about what he believes about food and how it should be prepared and eaten.

"If you want safe food, raise it yourself," he said to a round of applause.

Brown said earlier in the week he wanted a piece of homemade strawberry-rhubarb pie during his brief stay in Iowa. He'll have plenty to take back to Atlanta with him.

Andrea Lewerenz-Norris, 36, of Cedar Rapids, brought a homemade strawberry-rhubarb pie to the preshow reception. "What made him perk up was that it has a little bit of

lard in it," she said.

Lewerenz-Norris said she has been a longtime fan of Brown.

"He was the first TV guy who got me interested in cooking," she said.

Lewerenz-Norris' friend Stephanie Rex brought Brown a jar of her homemade strawberry-rhubarb jam. The Kirkwood Community College culinary arts program and Kathy's Pies also delivered pies to him.

■ Comments: (319) 398-5860; angie.holmes@sourcemedia.net

Jim Slosiarek photos/The Gazette

Author and television personality Alton Brown talks last night about a Jell-O recipe book at Theatre Cedar Rapids. Brown donated numerous cookbooks to the Cedar Rapids Public Library.

Author and television personality Alton Brown shakes hands with Kirkwood Community College culinary arts student Michelle Tiemessen (right) of New Hampton last night during a social hour.

Needs Assessment

The Banned Books Trading Card project was developed to meet three needs:

1. **Raise awareness of Banned Books Week in a fresh and unique way.** Lawrence Public Library (LPL) has long celebrated Banned Books Week in the manner that many libraries do—with a display of banned or challenged books and a program or two about censorship. For the week's 30th anniversary, we wanted to do something fresh and unique to heighten awareness of challenges to intellectual freedom. With a population of nearly 90,000 people, Lawrence, KS is a college town with a large contingent of academics, writers, readers, and artists. We felt that the message of Banned Books Week would resonate deeply if presented in a creative way.

2. **Engage the Lawrence arts community, both artists and arts organizations.** One of LPL's current goals is to build strategic partnerships with major community organizations and strong relationships with key demographic segments. By partnering with the Chamber of Commerce, we have strengthened our ties with the business community. Through programs and partnerships with the University of Kansas, we have reached out to university students and faculty. However, apart from offering gallery space, LPL had not directly engaged the local arts community—either individual artists or arts organizations—in many meaningful ways.

3. **Bring greater exposure to local artists and support the marketing of Lawrence as an arts destination.** Lawrence is a small city with big artistic talent. Through festivals, art walks, and designated arts districts, civic leaders are currently working to market Lawrence as a regional and national arts destination. As both a gateway to our community and a showcase for all of the talent within, LPL is well-positioned to support this civic and economic initiative.

Planning

While the idea had been simmering for a few years, planning began in June 2012, when the project was awarded a $1,000 Judith F. Krug Memorial Grant by the Freedom to Read Foundation (FTRF). The Friends of the Lawrence Public Library generously matched the grant, giving the project a total budget of $2,000.

Because LPL had never coordinated an arts competition, we asked the Lawrence Arts Center (LAC) for assistance in planning the initial phase. LAC provided insight into possible ways to engage artists, including commissioning seven well-known artists or commissioning one artist for all seven pieces. Due to budget constraints and a desire to reach out to artists of all ages and at all

From *Crash Course in Marketing for Libraries: Second Edition* by Susan W. Alman and Sara Gillespie Swanson. Santa Barbara, CA: Libraries Unlimited. Copyright © 2015.

stages of their careers, a community-wide Call for Artists was agreed upon and drafted by LPL with assistance from LAC. The only requirements for submission were:

- Artists had to live in Lawrence/Douglas County
- Artwork had to be inspired by a banned book or author
- Pieces had to be submitted on paper
- A brief Artist's Statement had to accompany the submission

The Call for Artists also detailed the selection process and the rewards for the chosen pieces. The selection jury was comprised of Brad Allen, LPL Director; Ben Ahlvers, LAC's Director of Exhibits; and Lucia Orth, a local author and library supporter. While no monetary reward was attached, the winning art would be reproduced as a trading card and featured in a week-long exhibit at LAC. All of the other submitted pieces would be exhibited in the LPL lobby and on the LPL website.

The Call for Artists went out in July and was publicized by LPL and by local arts organizations, including LAC, the Lawrence Arts Guild, the Lawrence Arts Commission, and area galleries and artists' collectives. By the deadline, we had received 46 entries from artists of all ages and degrees of experience—high school students, college students, and established artists. After three hours of deliberation, the jury chose seven pieces to be printed as trading cards.

After the art was selected, we reached out to local businesses to help produce high-quality cards. A local digital services company donated high-resolution scans of all seven pieces, and while there are several online sources for printing trading cards, we wanted to involve local businesses as much as possible and so contracted with a local printing company to produce the cards. The front of each card featured the art and the back was designed to have the look and feel of a trading card, with a background reminiscent of cardboard, "stats" about each book and artist, and the logos of all project partners at the bottom. 600 sets were printed, with 400 to be given away, 150 set aside for promotional giveaways, and 50 sets to be divided among the artists.

From *Crash Course in Marketing for Libraries: Second Edition* by Susan W. Alman and Sara Gillespie Swanson. Santa Barbara, CA: Libraries Unlimited. Copyright © 2015.

Implementation

Strategic execution was essential to the project's success and was designed to maximize word-of-mouth buzz and encourage visitors to the library every day during Banned Books Week. One card would be unveiled and distributed each day—300 at LPL and 100 at LAC. While previous days' cards would be distributed throughout the week if available, a limited run was printed. To guarantee a complete set, participants had to visit LPL or LAC every day. To build even more buzz, a "sneak peek" event was planned.

Two days before the start of Banned Books Week, we hosted a Final Fridays reception in our auditorium to unveil the seven winners and to launch the exhibit of all submissions. Final Fridays is a monthly downtown art walk where art lovers can stop by galleries to view art installations and mingle with artists. LPL usually participates with a small "punch and cookies" type reception, but for this event, we hosted a larger, after-hours affair with desserts from a local bakery and wine from a local vineyard.

Nearly 150 people attended, including four of the winning artists and several of the artists who had submitted pieces. The winning art was displayed in frames, with large format reproductions hung behind them and artists stationed nearby to chat with guests. Just outside the auditorium, the other 39 original pieces were displayed with artists standing nearby. Although the first card was not officially available until Sunday, there was a door prize drawing for 12 full sets of cards. The winners were thrilled to receive a complete set and helped to spread the word-of-mouth buzz about the project.

On Sunday, there was even more buzz, due to a front page feature article in the local newspaper, the *Lawrence Journal World* (LJW). We had hoped to have each day's card printed in the paper, but the budget precluded paid advertising. After sending a press release, we followed up by phone with the LJW and pitched the story. They not only agreed to print each day's card, they agreed to print them on the front page and develop a Sunday feature as well. This earned media helped sustain the buzz about the project throughout the week.

In addition to the front page of the paper, the plan for releasing each day's card included:

- A large format version of the card in the library lobby
- Card image on LPL website, Facebook page, and Twitter feed
- Card image on partner's websites and social media, including LAC and FTRF

The route to the service desk where the cards were distributed went past several points featuring information about banned books:

- The exhibit of all art submissions in the lobby, with the large format version of each day's card next to it

- "Cozy Up to a Banned Book" installation that encouraged people to sit down and peruse some banned books
- A large display of banned or challenged books with Banned Books Week buttons and bookmarks

On Sunday, staff recorded increased foot traffic, the lobby exhibit was crowded with viewers, numerous positive comments were posted on social media and just over 200 of the first day's 300 cards were distributed at LPL within 6 hours. This level of interest and participation continued all week long.

Creativity

Artistic creativity was central to the entire project—without great art, the cards would not have been as popular. The styles of art ran the spectrum—from the book jacket illustration for *Animal Farm* to the mixed-media piece for *Rabbit Run,* with an actual burned book cover. *Slaughterhouse Five* and *The Origin of Species* showcased two different stylistic approaches to digitally-native art. *The Call of the Wild* card showed off a talented teen artist. *Little Red Riding Hood* and 1984 represented two of the oldest and newest artistic forms—wood block printing and comic book illustration. The remaining 39 pieces also represented highly creative artwork and a variety of styles, making the lobby and online exhibits interesting and engaging.

The creative format for the project was part of the draw as well. Art trading cards have been popular for some time, but combining them with the message of intellectual freedom was a fresh approach that also provided great inspiration to the artists. Artists, art lovers, writers, and readers are groups that are all affected by censorship and challenges to artistic and intellectual freedom. Presenting the big ideas of this topic in the small format of an art trading card resonated with both artists and card collectors.

Creative social promotion played a key role in the project's success. Each day's card was posted on Facebook and Twitter with a call to action of "Get today's card before it's gone!" which reinforced the message that the cards were a limited run collector's item. Messages like "If you think today's card is great, wait until you see tomorrow's!" help build anticipation for the next day's card. As the week progressed, the number of likes, comments, shares, and retweets continually increased. LPL also leveraged the viral nature of social media by encouraging FTRF, LAC, and others to share the cards on their social media.

Evaluation

Based on the project's stated goals, it was an overwhelming success:

Raise awareness of Banned Books Week in a fresh and unique way. While it is nearly impossible to gauge the level of awareness before the cards were launched, it is clear that our community knows more about Banned Books Week now:

- Via the front page, the LJW's 16,000+ readers were exposed to the message of Banned Books Week every day that week.

- At LPL, increased foot traffic was registered all week long, and everyone who came in to get a card was surrounded with information about the freedom to read. The cards provided a teachable moment at the Reference Desk, as staff answered countless questions about why each book was banned or challenged.

- Our social media audience was exposed to the message of Banned Books Week. At the time, our Facebook following was approximately 3,000 and our Twitter following was around 2,800. The cards were seen by these followers and then shared by many of them. As a result of the viral nature of social media, in the course of the week, we gained nearly 100 new followers on both Facebook and Twitter.

- By week's end, we had given away more than 400 sets of cards, and everyone who received a set now possesses a permanent, hand-held reminder of Banned Books Week as well as a collection of beautiful artwork from Lawrence artists.

Engage the Lawrence arts community, both artists and arts organizations. Because of this project, LPL has new connections in the arts community. Local artists have a new perspective on LPL as a creative community center and many have already begun asking about submission deadlines for the 2013 cards. By including LAC, an anchor arts organization, in the project planning and execution, they shared in the positive PR and exposure associated with the project. By asking other area arts organizations to help publicize the project, we have new contacts at each of these organizations and are already planning new programs and other joint ventures.

Bring greater exposure to local artists and support the marketing of Lawrence as an arts destination. The project brought a great deal of attention to Lawrence artists, in both local and national media outlets:

- The LJW feature was picked up by the AP Wire, and appeared in newspapers in Seattle, Chicago, and elsewhere

- Via social media, the cards were discovered by national media outlets, including *Flavorwire, Vulture,* and *Huffington Post*
- Book-related outlets promoted the project, including *GalleyCat, BookRiot,* and Nancy Pearl's *Publisher's Weekly* column
- Library-related outlets featured the cards, including the *Library as Incubator* project

Beyond the three stated goals, the project created a few surprise outcomes that continue to raise awareness of challenges to intellectual freedom and bring greater exposure to local artists, well after the end of 2012's Banned Books Week.

Only an hour or so after the first card was released, we started receiving inquiries via email and social media from people well outside of the Lawrence area, asking if the cards were for sale. We had held back some cards for PR purposes and were initially open to mailing a few sets out to other libraries that might be interested. However, by Monday, national interest was so high that we needed to develop a different approach in order to meet demand.

To capitalize on national interest and on the week itself, we quickly set up a way for the cards to be purchased. Within one 24 hour period, we drafted an agreement with all seven artists for the sale of an additional run of cards, had an extra 1,000 cards printed, and set up a PayPal site for sales. Under the terms of the agreement, each artist receives 5% of every set sold with the rest going back to the library to cover costs of production, sales, and shipping. Although the cards went up for sale on Wednesday of Banned Books Week, we made it clear that Lawrence area residents could still get them for free during the week, and in fact made an additional 50 sets of free cards available at LPL. After Banned Books Week, cards were available for sale at the library as well.

As this application is being written, we are still selling cards via our website and at the Circulation Desk, months after Banned Books Week ended. So far, we have shipped nearly 800 sets to every state in the US, as well as Canada, Great Britain, Australia, and New Zealand. The sales of the cards have been a great by-product of the project, bringing continued exposure for the library and the artists and heightened awareness of Banned Books Week. Card sales have resulted in a modest, unexpected monetary benefit for the artists. For the library, the project has not only paid for itself, but card sales continue to bolster the marketing budget.

We have also received many inquiries from librarians around the country interested in replicating the project and creating cards themselves. We have shared our approach and process with numerous libraries and if only a few of them actually create cards this year, 2013 will see similar cards at libraries throughout the country, spreading the message of intellectual freedom and promoting local artists in many different communities. LPL is planning to make Banned Books Trading Cards an annual initiative and The Friends of the Library have already allocated funds for 2013 cards. We expect even more entries this year and with an annual Banned Books Trading Cards project, we look forward to continuing to deliver a big message in a small format.

Banned Books Trading Cards—Project Budget

All figures are rounded off and this budget snapshot is based on sales of 800 sets thus far.

Project Funds

Freedom to Read Foundation grant	$ 1,000.00
Friends of the Library matching grant	$ 1,000.00
Total	**$ 2,000.00**

Project Expenses

Original print run

600 sets of cards	$ 750.00
Large format versions for display	$ 200.00
Frames, foam core, exhibit materials	$ 275.00
Final Fridays reception	$ 250.00
Total	**$ 1,475.00**

Second print run

1,000 sets of cards	$ 465.00*
Shipping supplies	$ 75.00
Postage	$ 175.00
Payment to artists (35% of sales)	$ 1,960.00
Total	**$ 2,675.00**
Total expenses	**$ 4,150.00**

Project revenues

Total sales as of 2/2013	**$ 5,600.00**

Total profit for library as of 2/2013 **(Revenues minus expenses)**	**$ 1,450.00****

*The printer offered to sell us the overrun from the original printing at a discounted price.

**While the original project was seeded with grant money and cards were intended to be given away freely, the subsequent sales of the cards have provided an unexpected monetary benefit for the artists involved and a way to bolster the marketing budget for the library.

From *Crash Course in Marketing for Libraries: Second Edition* by Susan W. Alman and Sara Gillespie Swanson. Santa Barbara, CA: Libraries Unlimited. Copyright © 2015.

Appendix E

Sample Marketing Plan

Brand Statement

Mid-Continent Public Library provides unparalleled access to quality information.

Plan Purpose

The purpose of this plan is to help the Library communicate the new "Access Your World" brand to stakeholders both internal and external. Exposure to and understanding of the brand should be maximized through the combination of message and media.

Background

MCPL, and libraries in general, are at a pivotal time in their histories. Technology is greatly changing what we provide and how our communities interact with us. While most libraries have done a very admirable job in embracing this change, we have had less success at communicating the shift to our customers. Our library world is quickly shifting from physical to digital, but the general perception of the library as a warehouse of books remains entrenched. In the 2010 Online Computer Library Center (OCLC) study, *Perceptions of Libraries*, 75% of respondents said the word they most associate with libraries is "books." MCPL's own users have sent the same message in website polling and in surveys.

The library has identified the need to change that customer perception as the key to demonstrating relevance. Throughout customer surveys, focus groups, a literature review, and staff discussions, the concept of "access" kept surfacing when the discussion turned to what libraries truly offer. The branding team realized that this idea of "access" not only gets at the root of libraries do, but also begins to tie together the wide variety of products and services we offer.

In addition, the concept of "access" is really an idea that has animated MCPL since its inception. When individual library systems and voters from Clay, Jackson, and Platte counties came together almost five decades ago to create MCPL, the reason was to provide a level of access none could provide on their own. When the Library undertook a major building campaign in the eighties and nineties, the goal was to provide access to communities who previously were without. And in the early 21st century, the Library began working on a project to put smaller, automated libraries in places where citizens already conducted their daily lives. The goal was to provide access.

Reorienting public perception toward the idea that libraries provide access and not books is a difficult proposition. The idea that libraries equal books is highly ingrained. However, it is not too far a leap to recognize that the content provided by the library is more important than the paper and ink visible there. It is possible, but it requires focus. We must remind users and non-users alike that libraries are portals for ideas, not warehouses of books. More broadly, we must change our focus from libraries as places to a single entity that provides information in a variety of media (including physical places). We can do these things through consistent communication of our central concept—access.

Key Audiences and Messages

There are multiple audiences in this rebranding campaign. The messages required for these individual groups are related, but include differentiations that make each unique.

External Audiences	Key Message
Community Members	Libraries aren't just books.
Customers	We have more to offer you.
Non-customers	The Library has services to improve your life.
Community Leaders	The Library remains as relevant as ever.

In addition, there are two distinct internal audiences who need to buy in to the brand message before we can make it successful with those external audiences.

Internal Audiences	Key Message
Staff	We are providers of access.
Board of Trustees	Access keeps the Library relevant.

Branding Goals

Goal 1: Change the public's perception of the Library from the traditional "warehouse of books" model to the place where ideas are shared and imagination is stimulated.

Goal 2: Use the expanded perception of libraries from Goal 1 to educate customers about non-traditional library services and increase their use and value.

Goal 3: Ensure that the brand becomes an integral part of the Library's culture, not just a marketing effort.

The Brand Tagline and Logo

Tagline

The "access" brand will take shape around a layered tag message. The reason for this format instead of a simple tagline is that the varying text can be more meaningful and requires the reader to engage in a way that a tagline does not. The layering will consist of a root message and a series of secondary messages. Each of these messages will be a call to action.

Root Message—Access Your World

The root message is intended to communicate the essence of the brand and imply broad offerings. The series of secondary messages are meant to complement the root message, but should imply more specific benefits associated with varied library services. Some examples are:

Service	Message
Book Clubs	Access Community
Job Search Resources	Access Opportunity
Summer Reading Program	Access Literacy
Tech Classes	Access Innovation

A list of Access messages will be developed. While it will be an evolving list, certain words will be required for certain services.

An important aspect of the layered message is consistency in appearance. In four-color applications, the word "Access" should always appear in black or white while the rest of the phrase appears in a vibrant color. This places the focus on the idea being accessed, and allows the "Access" word to function as a consistent brand element. In black and white applications, the secondary piece of the phrase should appear in grey to separate it from the word "Access."

Logo

The traditional Mid-Continent Public Library "book" logo will not change. While this may seem counterintuitive when we are attempting to change the image of the Library away from books, it is critical that the rebranding process not become an exercise in changing the logo. Logo changes often take center stage in rebranding processes and obscure the fundamental organizational changes that are necessary to truly rebrand. The logo will, whenever possible, appear with an access message.

Brand Communication

Internal Communication Tools

Board of Trustees Branding Presentation—This presentation will be the critical first step in launching the brand. An engaged and supportive board is critical to ensuring the organizational change necessary to rebrand.

Staff "Accessibility" Training Session—A half-day training session will teach staff members about the brand, encourage them to take ownership of the brand, and explain how they can carry the brand to Library customers.

Staff "Access Specialist" T-Shirts—These t-shirts will be a persistent reminder that the true work we perform at the library is providing access. It will also communicate to customers that the Library staff they are working with are experts that can help them access information and ideas.

External Communication Tools

Access Passes—Library cards are key components of a library customer's relationship with the library, but they are highly associated with checking out books. We will rename ours "Access Passes" to highlight the idea that the card is a key to all the Library offers.

Access Guides—The live programming guides will become "Access Guides." They will better align with brand by grouping branches who share customers together so that those customers are able to see wider offerings.

Digital Libraries—The virtual branch, app, and email newsletter will all be updated with the Access branding. In addition, we will emphasize greater communication and interaction on digital assets. This will take the form of blog posts from the Library Director, an active comment response policy, and an effort to include customer created content.

Social Media—A critical piece of increasing openness and communication with customers is an emphasis on social media. The Library will develop an enhanced plan for posting and interacting on social media. We will set goals for social media activities and ensure communication remains open on all social media sites.

Advertising—A mix of traditional media will be utilized for the rollout of the branding effort. In addition, a series of ads will be built cross-format to communicate with non-library customers about "wow factor" library services that grab attention because they are unexpected. In addition, when non-users are exposed to multiple ads, the variety communicates the breadth of what can be accessed at the Library.

Advertising Message Mix Matrix					
	Billboard	**Print**	**Online**	**Radio**	**Television**
Job Search Resources	X	X	X	X	
Homework Help	X	X	X		X
eBooks	X	X	X		
Digital Music	X	X	X	X	X
Online Learning	X	X	X		

Collateral Material—All promotional items purchased after adoption of this plan will carry the Access message. Some of the more popular items affected are coffee mugs, temporary tattoos, and miniature Frisbees.

Budget

The budget for this marketing effort is broken into three categories: internal costs, external costs, and in-kind support. The internal costs are primarily comprised of staff time dedicated to each item. The external costs will be provided by a special allocation from the Board of Trustees. The in-kind support is expected free media time donated by partners.

	Internal Cost	**External Cost**	**In-Kind**	**Total**
Campaign Creation	$34,800			$34,800
Staff Training	$35,200			$35,200
Media Buys and Production Costs	$75,000		$15,000	$90,000
Total				$160,000

Evaluation

Success for this plan will be measured three ways:

Measure 1—Media Performance. We will measure both total and unique impressions. In addition, we will measure total frequency. We would like to have 1 million unique impressions throughout the campaign and a combined frequency of 7 messages per unique impression.

Measure 2—Growth in Use of Promoted Services. A successful campaign will see growth among the promoted services of 25%. This number was developed from the track record of previous smaller media pushes for library services. These services aren't widely known among the larger public, so significant growth opportunity should be available.

Measure 3—Stakeholder Receptivity. Quantitatively, this can be measured by the growth in the number of customers who identify "access" as the word they most associate with the library. That number was 5% in the previous survey. We would like to see a doubling to 10% a year after the brand is introduced. Qualitatively, we would like good feedback from stakeholders about the brand and the Library. While this is subjective, positive anecdotes can indicate a broader positive shift.

Appendix F

Sample Promotional Materials

Welcome to
MT. LEBANON
PUBLIC
LIBRARY

Mt. Lebanon Public Library was founded in 1932. It is governed by the Library Board of Trustees and funded by the Municipality of Mt. Lebanon, with significant additional funding from both the Allegheny Regional Asset District and from the Commonwealth of Pennsylvania.

:more books, movies, ideas, fun, family, resources, programs, culture, authors, visionaries, characters, connections, inspirations, entertainment, business, science, workshops, learning, events, new beginnings, knowledge, searches, members, stories, languages, friends

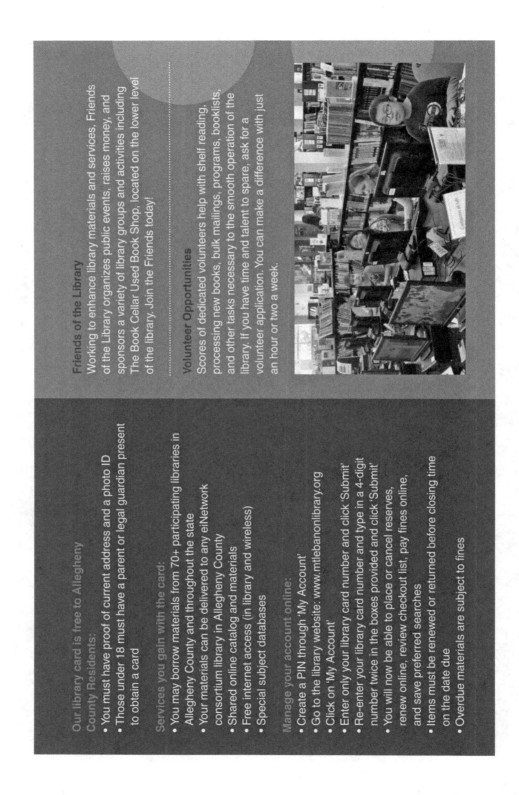

Our library card is free to Allegheny County Residents:

- You must have proof of current address and a photo ID
- Those under 18 must have a parent or legal guardian present to obtain a card

Services you gain with the card:

- You may borrow materials from 70+ participating libraries in Allegheny County and throughout the state
- Your materials can be delivered to any eiNetwork consortium library in Allegheny County
- Shared online catalog and materials
- Free internet access (in library and wireless)
- Special subject databases

Manage your account online:

- Create a PIN through 'My Account'
- Go to the library website: www.mtlebanonlibrary.org
- Click on 'My Account'
- Enter only your library card number and click 'Submit'
- Re-enter your library card number and type in a 4-digit number twice in the boxes provided and click 'Submit'
- You will now be able to place or cancel reserves, renew online, review checkout list, pay fines online, and save preferred searches
- Items must be renewed or returned before closing time on the date due
- Overdue materials are subject to fines

Friends of the Library

Working to enhance library materials and services, Friends of the Library organizes public events, raises money, and sponsors a variety of library groups and activities including The Book Cellar Used Book Shop, located on the lower level of the library. Join the Friends today!

Volunteer Opportunities

Scores of dedicated volunteers help with shelf reading, processing new books, bulk mailings, programs, booklists, and other tasks necessary to the smooth operation of the library. If you have time and talent to spare, ask for a volunteer application. You can make a difference with just an hour or two a week.

Adult Department

Adult Services

- Adult summer reading program
- Art gallery and rotating displays
- Book discussion groups
- Gadget workshops
- Home delivery service for disabled patrons
- Individual computer instruction
- Interlibrary loans on material not owned by county libraries (additional fees may apply)
- Language groups
- Meeting rooms

- Online databases
- Printers and copy machines
- Document scanners
- Quiet study rooms
- Readers' advisory
- Reference assistance in library, phone, online
- Test center (online resources and proctoring)
- Free WiFi and computers with Internet Access

Special Collections

- ESL— English as a second language materials
- Foundation Directory Online and GrantSelect
- Great Courses and Modern Scholar
- Job Bank and Career collections

- Large print books
- Mt. Lebanon historical information
- Play scripts
- Reference items
- Special needs resources for parents of children with special needs

General Collections

- Books, magazines, and newspapers
- Downloadable audio and e-books
- DVDs and videos
- Kindles and Nooks to borrow
- Language CDs, USBs, online databases

- Music CDs
- Playaways — spoken books on MP3 players and videos
- Special subject databases
- Unabridged books on CD

Teen Services

Programs

- Craft and holiday programs
- Movies, gaming, and tailgate parties
- Otaku—Lebo Japanese pop culture group

- Teen read week contests and programs
- Teen summer reading program
- Teen library lock-ins

Young Adult General Collections

- Books on CD and MP3 players
- Music CDs
- Study/homework resource center
- Teen reading lists for school and pleasure

- Wide variety of fiction and non-fiction books, graphic novels, and teen magazines

Children's Library

The Children's Library serves children from birth through eighth grade, parents, teachers, and other caregivers.

Storytimes
- Book Babies (birth - 2 years)
- Storytime for 2s and 3s (ages 2 and 3)
- Wild About Books (4 years - 6 years)
- Pajama Storytime (ages 3 - 7)
- And more!

Programs
- Book clubs for school-age kids
- Chess club
- Family programs
- Lego club
- Kidslit book club for adults
- Monthly craft Saturdays
- Mother/daughter and father/son book clubs
- Summer reading programs
- Tail Wagging Tutors (read to a dog)

Services for Children and Parents
- Babysitter bags — Take one of these along to your next babysitting gig. Books, videos, crafts, game ideas, and more!
- Express bags — Five age-appropriate books selected for children ages birth - 2; 2 - 4; and 4 - 6. Quick and easy!
- Grandparent bags — Books, music, movies, magazines, and more for visiting grandchildren.
- Math, science, holiday, and puppet kits
- Books and related educational toys or puppets
- Sick day comfort kits — Home from school for the day? Give us a call and we'll pull together a bag full of fun.
- Vacation bags — Packed with reading and listening fun for the trip.
- Book and author recommendations
- Booklists by age and subject
- Born to Read — Bring a photo of your baby (newborn -18 months) to the library and receive a baby reader starter kit.
- Displays — Do you have a collection of dinosaurs, dolls, dogs, or other cool stuff? Share it with us in our display case.
- Reference assistance and homework help
- Library tours

For Daycares, Extended Day, Homeschoolers, Scout Groups, Teachers, and Other Groups
- In library and outreach programs — Storytelling, book talks, special programs
- Library tours
- Parent-Teacher resource sections
- Preparation of special booklists
- Storytime-to-go kits — Theme-related books, CD, video, and puppets

Electronic Communications:
KidsRead Listserve Email
Follow us on Twitter:
http://twitter.com/MLPLKids
Links to each are on
www.mtlebanonlibrary.org/kids

From *Crash Course in Marketing for Libraries: Second Edition* by Susan W. Alman and Sara Gillespie Swanson. Santa Barbara, CA: Libraries Unlimited. Copyright © 2015.

The Library provides:

- 170,000+ items for your use
- Book discussion groups and book reviews
- Computer classes
- Email online newsletters and other electronic communications
- Family programs
- Full accessibility and adaptive devices for persons with disabilities (furniture, computers, equipment)
- Lectures, workshops, concerts, and other quality programming
- Municipal, community, and voter information
- Summer reading programs for children, teens, and adults
- And more!

Library Hours:

Monday — Thursday
9 AM — 9 PM
Friday — Saturday
9 AM — 5 PM
Sunday — 1PM - 5 PM

16 Castle Shannon Blvd.
Pittsburgh PA 15228-2252
Phone: 412-531-1912
info@mtlebanonlibrary.org
www.mtlebanonlibrary.org

Electronic Communications:
Books-Bytes-Buzz online library newsletter
Follow us on: f flickr ꭹ

Links to each are on www.mtlebanonlibrary.org

"Just Jeans in January"

Libraries throughout the Lackawanna County Library System are collecting used adult <u>blue jeans in good condition</u> for Clarks Summit State Hospital patients the month of January. They need:

ADULT-SIZE JEANS clean and in good condition. All sizes are fine.

Drop them here before February 1.

Mt. Lebanon Chairity

- . . . . How many chairs were you able to have decorated and auctioned off? . . . In the end, about 70 chairs were auctioned off.

- . . . . Did you hire an auctioneer or do a silent auction?. . . . Silent auction

- . . . . How did you go about recruiting artists to decorate the chairs?. . . . Local press and usual library means of communication to the community as well as contacting school art teachers and art groups. We also had about five staff members participate.

- . . . . Did you offer anything to the artists to help persuade them to participate (such as a percentage of the final auction price) or were they willing to do this gratis?. . . . Gratis. They paid for all materials, too.

- . . . . What sorts of paperwork did you have the artists fill out when they agreed to decorate a chair?. . . . Attached sample of chair check-out log and other related print materials.

- . . . . About how much money did the library bring in from your chair auction?. . . . About $7700 was raised from 70 chairs. $40 was the minimum bid.

From *Crash Course in Marketing for Libraries: Second Edition* by Susan W. Alman and Sara Gillespie Swanson. Santa Barbara, CA: Libraries Unlimited. Copyright © 2015.

Appendix G

Sample Annual Appeal

2013

Avon Grove Library Annual Appeal

Learn, Grow, Dream and Imagine @ Your Library®

A library enhances the quality of life for everyone!

"A public library is an important social institution that provides much needed resources – education and training, job search resources, and Internet access for applying for jobs and social services, among many, many other services – for patrons and communities." (Jaeger, et al.)

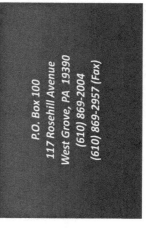

P.O. Box 100
117 Rosehill Avenue
West Grove, PA 19390
(610) 869-2004
(610) 869-2957 (Fax)

Our library programs include:

- Family Night Holiday Specials
- Preschool Storytimes
- Baby Lap-Sit Series
- Raise-A-Reader Series
- Avon Grove Girls
- Lego Club
- Story hour at Starbucks
- Summer Reading
- Family Activity Nights
- Teen Mystery Night, Anime Club, Teen Drawing Studio
- Science in the Summer
- Outreach to Summer Schools in Conjunction with Migrant Education
- Ongoing Outreach Programs to Area Preschools and Daycares
- Home School Educational Classes
- Kick-off Events for Major Programs
- Avon Grove Library Adult Book Club
- Adult Workshops on Current Topics of Interest
- Participation in the Statewide "One Book, Every Child" Program
- Adult Quilting & Craft Book Club
- Outreach Activities During Community Events

For More Information & A Calendar of Events, Visit:

www.avongrovelibrary.org

A Lifetime of Learning

Now is the time to look forward and embark on a lifetime of literacy for the whole family. A public library offers the resources and programs that enrich and educate our community residents, regardless of age or economic means.

Libraries promote basic literacy

In 2012, the Avon Grove Library offered **662** programs for children and adults. Our professional staff strives hard to plan and implement educational classes that promotes early literacy concepts, fosters skill development, and seeks to inspire the love of reading for all children. Exposure to quality literature in a fun and inviting environment helps build a lifelong reading habit.

Libraries build communities

People gather at libraries to find and share information, as well as engage in community meetings and discussions. Last year, **123,563** people walked through our doors. More than **22,000** people attended library programs. By connecting people from all walks of life, public libraries promote open communication and unity.

Libraries provide crucial resources and promote information literacy

The Avon Grove Library provides more than **51,500** items to the public. More than 4,800 items were added to the collection, including new books on CD, music CDs and DVDs. Circulation rose 14% over the prior year. More than **161,000** items were checked out by area residents. This was the highest percentage increase of all the libraries in Chester County.

Why Your Support is Needed

2012 Budget Income

- State
- County
- Municipalities
- Fines & Fees
- Community Funds
- Other

Approximately 20% of the library's operational budget comes directly from our local residents. Your gifts help us remain in service to the community.

"Whatever the cost of our libraries, the price is cheap compared to that of an ignorant nation."
- Walter Cronkite

Saving You Time & Money

Using the Chester County Library System homepage at: www.ccls.org, you can:

- View the online catalog for all 18 libraries in Chester County
- Place holds on the titles that you want
- Check your record and renew items
- Download free audio books & e-books
- Access authoritative information from our numerous online databases

Many Ways of Giving

- Make a personal contribution
- Support our annual fundraising event
- Make a gift in honor of someone else
- Ask your employer about a matching gift or corporate sponsorship
- Volunteer your services and/or special talents
- Ask your clubs or local organizations to make a donation
- Become a Library Board member
- Join the Friends of the Avon Grove Library
- Leave a legacy or bequeath for the future

Most of All.....
- Come to the public library often to experience our wonderful programs and informational resources

From *Crash Course in Marketing for Libraries: Second Edition* by Susan W. Alman and Sara Gillespie Swanson. Santa Barbara, CA: Libraries Unlimited. Copyright © 2015.

Dear Friend and Neighbor,

From my earliest memories, before I knew how to read, I recall my mother taking me to our local library, where I would select books that my parents would then read to me before bedtime.

As time passed, I would find books that I would attempt to read by myself; I couldn't wait to start reading. It was more than just the desire to be more grown up, it was the desire to have my own, greater access to the story, and to someone else's view of the world, and often a perspective that was new to me.

As I grew older, I found that I loved to explore the shelves of the library, and I often found books on topics for which I had never contemplated looking. Through exploring and discovering the narratives of others, I found that I was able to broaden, deepen, and refine my own life's narrative and sense of self.

When I see the tremendous energy and enthusiasm of patrons—*of every age*—at our own Avon Grove Library, I am excited; the library appears to be an essential element in the narrative of the lives of so many of us. The free access to everything from the classics to the newest bestsellers, eBooks, music and magazines, makes our library a wonderful resource, and I am always amazed that it offers so much with such a limited budget.

Last year, the Avon Grove Library welcomed 123,500 patrons. Our circulation increased 14% (the highest percentage increase of any Chester County library), with over 161,000 library materials checked out! These items were not only books, but also audio CDs, DVDs, music discs, magazines, journals, and even Nooks with pre-loaded titles. Additionally, our Children's Department hosted 591 lively events, encouraging the lifelong path of learning and exploration for more than 20,000 of our children.

Through the slim budgets of recent years, the Avon Grove Library has thrived, in large part as a result of your generosity and that of so many of our neighbors. Your tax deductible donation to the **Annual Appeal Fund Drive** directly supports all of our wonderful programs and services, and keeps our collection of books and movies current.

On behalf of the entire Board of Trustees, I thank you for your support. An envelope is enclosed for your convenience. May I also ask that you consider making the library part of your life's overall narrative by remembering the library in your estate plans.

Thank you!

Sincerely,

Library Board President

From *Crash Course in Marketing for Libraries: Second Edition* by Susan W. Alman and Sara Gillespie Swanson. Santa Barbara, CA: Libraries Unlimited. Copyright © 2015.

Appendix H

Sample Annual Reports

Benicia Public Library
2012-2013
Annual Report

The Benicia Public Library contributes to the success of our diverse community by being a vital center of learning, communication, culture and enjoyment.

Benicia Public Library

Phone: 707-746-4343
www.BeniciaLibrary.org

Did you know?

The Library has **99,608** items, including magazines, newspapers, DVDs, music CDs, books on CD, novels and non-fiction books for all ages plus an additional **13,358** electronic books and downloadable audiobooks. * There were **17,925** library card holders in Benicia or **66%** of the population, and **3,671** children ages 5-14, have library cards! * The library endeavors to have something for everyone: if a specific item is not available, we can borrow items for you from another library. Last year we borrowed **61,920** items from other libraries. Suggestions for additions to the collection and comments are always welcome! * **220,798** visitors came to the library in 2012-2013: accessing public computers and the wireless system **62,709** times and checking out **474,472** items. This is equivalent to every person in Benicia checking out **17.46** items during the year. * **Measure B**, a 1/8 cent sales tax approved by the citizens of Solano County in 1998, contributed over **$681,000** in **2012-13** for books and materials, children's programming and more open hours for the library. Every dollar of sales tax spent in Benicia helps our Library.

Thank you for supporting the library by shopping "Benicia First"!

Benicia Public Library
150 East "L" Street
Benicia, California 94510

Phone: 707-746-4343
Fax: 707-747-8122
www.BeniciaLibrary.org

Rev. 11-22-13

New Services in 2012-2013

Downloadable books, E-books, and Playaway devices. Benicia Public Library users can now download audiobooks, e-books, and more for free — anytime, anywhere. A shared collection of hundreds of popular fiction and non-fiction items are available online through the e-books tab on the Library's website. In addition, the library has a total of 32 fiction and non-fiction Nook e-book readers, and many Playaway digital audioplayers, available for your use.

Discover and Go. Benicia residents now have access to free and low-cost museum passes that can be downloaded and printed from their home computers. Anyone with a SNAP (Solano Napa and Partners) library card can use the passes found on the Benicia Library website. Admission with each pass varies, with some locations offering family passes and others offering group discounts. The passes can be printed at home, so no pickup or return to the library is necessary.

Poet Laureate Lois Requist. Benicia's fourth Poet Laureate started her term in July 2012, continuing some of the excellent work done by her predecessor, Ronna Leon. Lois has created a synergy for poetry readings with the events surrounding "Art Walk", as she continues to make poetry accessible to the community.

Books for Book clubs. The Library will now loan sets of books for your book club. Each set has 8 -10 copies. One person will check out the set for their group and has 60 days to read and return them.

Trivia Bee. Save the date: Feb. 22, 2014
This year's theme: The Maltese Falcon!

129

Benicia Public Library 2012-2013 Annual Report

The Year in Review

Finances for the City of Benicia continued to "bounce along the bottom" as an unexpected property tax decline created a new obstacle for city revenues. Nevertheless, the Library completed projects and piloted new programs aligned with our mission and vision as well as with the community's needs.

Benicia—This Place Has History

In March 2013, the Library received a grant for $15,000 to pilot a new program. Working with the museum and the historical society as well as other community organizations, the Library will soon start placing QR (Quick Read) codes on buildings of historical importance. Look for these QR codes in the community, as the project will continue through the next year.

World Language Collection

The world language collection of children's books provided through a generous grant from the Valero Benicia Refinery will expand our early reader's collection and increase the number of books for children in multiple languages. In addition, grant funds allowed us to add a database called Little Pim that can teach children how to speak world languages.

E-books and E-book Readers

During the last few years, the library started to purchase e-books for our readers. The library now has 32 Nook readers with books for children and young adults, books in Spanish, as well as adult fiction and non-fiction books. Six Kindles were also purchased by the library. These provide a text-to-speech option, so users can listen as well as read on these devices.

Library Elf

If you have been searching for a way to use texting to keep track of your library requests and due dates, take a look at a new option called Library Elf.

Measure L — THANK YOU AGAIN!

Measure L provided an extension of the current 1/8 cent sales tax established by Measure B in 1998. In June 2012, Measure L passed by 82% in Benicia: this funding will allow all libraries in Solano County to move into the future with a strong, solid funding base. In Benicia, these funds pay for 33% of Library operations. Thank you for your support of our Library!!!

Library Funding 2012-2013

- City General Fund (59%)
- Sales Tax (33%)
- Friends (4%)
- Foundation, grants & reserves (1%)
- Literacy funding (City's contribution 2%)

Benicia Public Library
150 East "L" Street
Benicia, California 94510

Phone: 707-746-4343
Fax: 707-747-8122
www.BeniciaLibrary.org

Bringing art and culture to the community

The Benicia Public Library contributes to the success of our diverse community by being a vital center of learning, communication, culture and enjoyment.

In 2010, the Arts and Culture Commission was formed with library staff assisting the commission to achieve its goals. During 2012-13, the Commission completed a Public Art Program designed to create a process for public art to be placed in the community.

Approved by the City Council as Resolution 12–107, the program addresses the requirements for design, placement, maintenance, donations, and purchases of temporary and permanent public art.

Assisted by these guidelines, the Public Art Committee started to work on a conceptual design for a piece of glass and metal to be placed at the community center. The City's Community Sustainability Commission recommended grant funds to help with the project, and the piece will continue through the public art policy process during 2013-14.

Library Events, 2012-13

* Diablo Regional Concert Band *
* Celebration of the Library's 20th year of library service on East L Street *
* Annual pumpkin carving contest *
* Teddy Bear Sleepover *
* Ramana Vieira—Portuguese Fado Concert *
* Marion Coleman / Quilting display *

2013 Librarian's Annual Report

Mission Statement:

The Avon Grove Library provides materials, services and programming designed to meet the diverse educational, recreational, and cultural needs of the community. It supports universal access to information, inspires the love of reading, and promotes literacy and lifelong learning.

Service Area:

The Avon Grove Public Library, first established in 1874, is located in the borough of West Grove. The library, situated in Southern Chester County, currently serves more than 30,080 individuals, primarily in the Avon Grove School District. This district includes the West Grove and Avondale Boroughs, and the townships of Franklin, Penn, New London, London Britain, and London Grove. Since this library is a member of the Chester County Library System, it also distributes materials to other parts of the county via an interlibrary delivery service.

Highlights of the Year

The Avon Grove Library had another very successful year in the areas of programs, materials, and services. Some of the major accomplishments include

Materials:

We added 6,415 new items to the collection, including additional books on CD and current release DVDs. Due to space limitations and obsolete or worn materials, weeding was extensive. 3,207 items were deleted. Circulation of the total collection rose 5%, with 168,885 checkouts to Chester County residents. 64% of these checkouts went to residents in Avon Grove Library's designated service area. For comparison data, please see charts & graphs below.

Technology:

The library currently provides 13 computers for public use. More than 9,000 individuals used our public computers in 2013. In addition, many customers access our wireless network directly from the library facility on a daily basis.

The library also circulates seven Nooks, all packaged with popular titles, to the public. One Sony e-reader is also available. The staff provides one-on-one training in the use of these portable e-readers.

The Avon Grove Library continues to maintain and update its individual website at: www .avongrovelibrary.org. In addition, the library continues to maintain its organizational Facebook, Blog and Twitter accounts.

Programs:

The library offers numerous educational programs to the public. In 2013, the library hosted 778 programs sessions for children with an attendance of 21,739. The library also hosted 73 adult programs. More than 1,000 individuals attended these sessions. Programs that occurred include:

- Avon Grove Girls
- Family Night Holiday Specials
- Preschool Story Times
- Baby Lap-Sit Series
- Wee Ones Story time
- Story Hour at Starbucks
- Summer Reading with guest performances
- Summer Outreach at Dansko Corporation
- Teen Mystery Night
- Science in the Summer
- Outreach to Summer Schools in Conjunction with Migrant Education
- Migrant Education Year Round Saturday School
- Lego Club
- Mother Daughter Book Club
- Arts and Stories Program
- Star Wars Extravaganza
- Ongoing Outreach Programs to Area Preschools and Daycares

> Story times at Avon Grove School District Elementary Schools
> Kick-off Events for Major Programs
> Book Signings for children and adults
> Participation in Chester County Library System "One Book" & CC-READS
> Adult Quilting & Craft Book Club
> Adult Book Club
> Outreach Activities during community events

Additional Services:

In an effort to reach the residents residing near the state of Delaware, the library continued to offer outreach services at a satellite location in the London Britain Township building. This site allows local residents to peruse a small collection of items, get a library card, place material requests, and pick up items. This outreach building, located on Good Hope Road in Landenberg, Pennsylvania, is open on Wednesdays from 6 to 8 PM.

Government Funding:

The Avon Grove Library received a modest increase in State funds in 2013. State funds increased by $2,569. County funds dropped by $313. The local support from our designated municipalities increased by $13,514. The following townships increased their allocations to the library: Franklin, London Grove, New London and Penn.

Fundraising & Grants:

The Friends of the Library, in coordination with the Library Board of Trustees, hosted their first annual *Once Upon a Time . . .* event held at the Youth Garage in West Grove. The event, which featured a silent auction, live music and a wide variety of food and drinks, raised approximately $8,000. All proceeds were used to support the children's literacy programs held at the library.

The Avon Grove Library received one corporate grant from Capital One in the amount of $15,000 to support the children's literacy programs.

Major Board Accomplishments for 2013:

Library trustees participated in the annual fundraising event, monitored budget and fiscal management policies, developed a new set of bylaws, monitored the achievement of library goals and objectives, worked on the new strategic plan, attended CCLS events, including the Legislative Breakfast, and advocated the mission of the library throughout the local community.

From *Crash Course in Marketing for Libraries: Second Edition* by Susan W. Alman and Sara Gillespie Swanson. Santa Barbara, CA: Libraries Unlimited. Copyright © 2015.

Friends of the Avon Grove Library:

The 2013 Officers included: Terri Ahern, President; Hope Yarbrough, Secretary; and Jacquelyn Mace, Treasurer. At the end of 2013, there were 33 total members. A membership drive is ongoing. The Friends donated $8,000 to the library. This amount was used to fund the children's literacy programs.

To gain this support for the library, the Friends presented the *Once Upon a Time . . .* event held at the Youth Garage in West Grove, hosted the annual book sale, and sold tote bags. The tote bags were designed based on entries submitted by elementary aged children. The winner of the contest was Joseph Yarbrough. Bookmarks were produced to capture the art work of every child who submitted an entry.

Due to limited membership, the Friends are concentrating their efforts on larger fundraising activities for the forthcoming year.

Charts & Graphs

Circulation

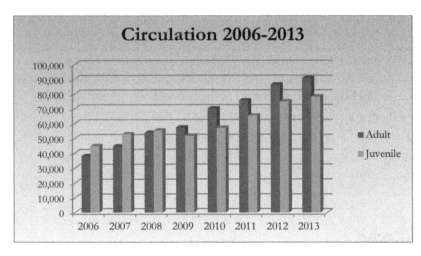

	2006	2007	2008	2009	2010	2011	2012	2013
Adult Circulation	38,125	44,574	53,792	57,315	70,078	75,536	86,329	90,768
Juvenile Circulation	44,847	52,739	55,360	51,715	57,146	65,351	74,820	78,117
Total Circulation	82,972	97,313	101,071	108,859	127,224	140,887	161,141	168,885
% Change from prior year	+24%	+17%	+4%	+8%	+17%	+11%	+14%	+5%

Charts & Graphs

General Attendance

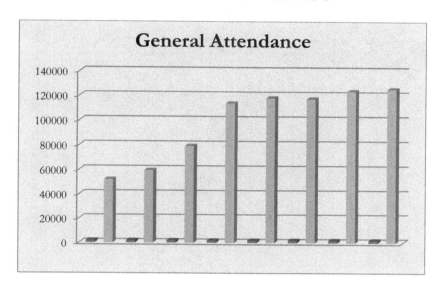

	2006	2007	2008	2009	2010	2011	2012	2013
General Attendance	52,028	59,434	79,202	113,731	118,088	117,369	123,563	125,353
% Change From prior year	+16%	+14%	+33%	+58%	+4%	-1%	+5%	+1%

Charts & Graphs

Children's & Young Adult Programming

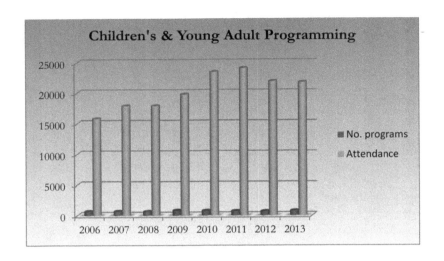

	2006	2007	2008	2009	2010	2011	2012	2013
Number of Programs	678	650	833	777	712	689	591	778
% Change from prior year	+15	-4%	+28%	-7%	-9%	-3%	-14%	+32%
Attendance	17,909	17,909	19,781	23,458	24,094	21,016	20,473	21,739
% change from prior year	+13%	0%	+10%	+19%	+3%	-9%	-9%	+6%

Charts & Graphs

Adult Programming

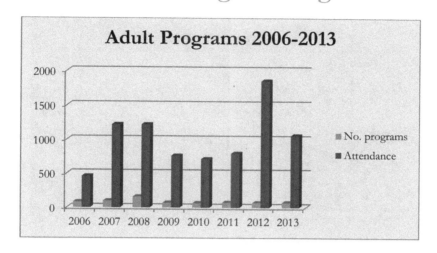

	2006	2007	2008	2009	2010	2011	2012	2013
Number of Programs	85	100	161	71	68	76	71	73
% Change from prior year	+44%	+18%	+61%	-56%	-6%	+12%	-5%	+3%
Attendance	460	1,221	1,954	763	713	795	1,851	1,058
% change from prior year	-32%	+165%	+60%	-61%	-7%	+12%	+133%	-43%

Charts & Graphs

Collection Size

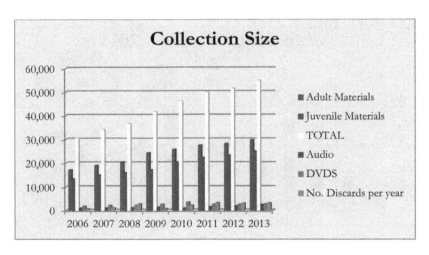

	2006	2007	2008	2009	2010	2011	2012	2013
Adult Materials	17,214	19,067	20,551	24,387	25,834	27,570	28,232	29,873
Juvenile Materials	13,365	15,051	16,068	17,307	20,345	22,303	23,287	24,997
TOTAL	30,579	34,118	36,619	41,694	46,179	49,873	51,519	54,870
Audio	1,019	1,087	1,255	1,439	1,019	1,550	2,039	2,595
DVDs	1,815	2,198	2,267	2,685	3,589	2,656	2,602	2,851
No. discards per year	717	1,195	2,880	861	2,298	3,339	3,123	3,207

Charts & Graphs

Reference Questions & Computer Usage

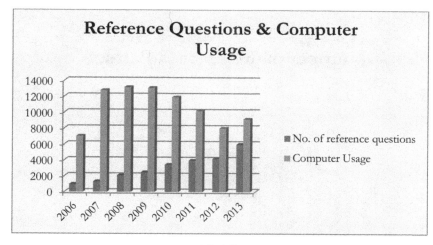

	2006	2007	2008	2009	2010	2011	2012	2013
No, of Reference Questions	991	1,314	2,087	2,472	3,420	3,954	4,170	6,002
% Change from prior year	+23%	+33%	+59%	+18%	+38%	+16%	+5%	+44%
Computer Usage	7,025	12,755	13,149	13,054	11,875	10,361	8,001	9,146
% Change from prior year	+72%	+82%	+3%	->1%	-9%	-14%	-21%	+14%

Charts & Graphs

Number of Active Registered Patrons

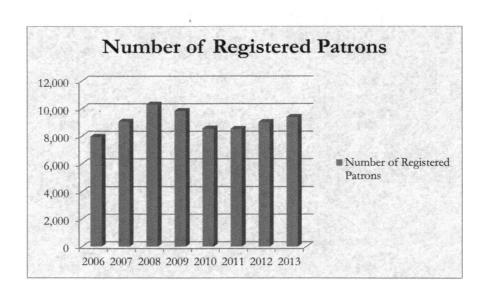

	2006	2007	2008	2009	2010	2011	2012	2013
Number of Registered Patrons	7,961	9,063	10,305	9,841	8,559	8,527	9,034	9,396

Charts & Graphs

State & County Funding

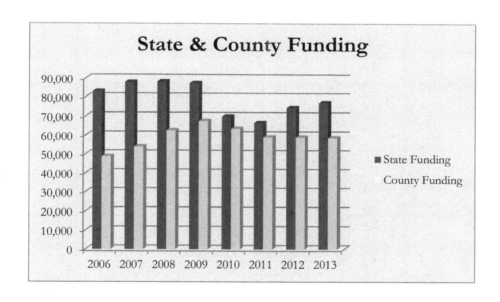

	2006	2007	2008	2009	2010	2011	2012	2013
State Funding	83,037	87,943	88,314	87,388	69,902	66,701	74,439	76,998
County Funding	48,748	54,054	62,704	67,577	63,609	59,055	59,256	58,742

Charts & Graphs

Local Municipal Funding

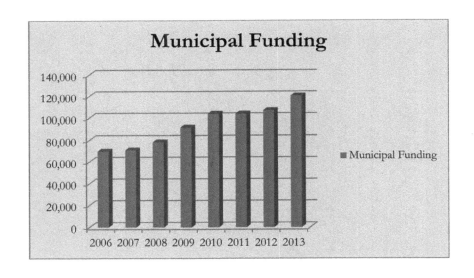

	2006	2007	2008	2009	2010	2011	2012	2013
Municipal Funding	69,844	70,844	78,344	91,527	103,810	103,810	106,752	120,266

Charts & Graphs

Budget Income

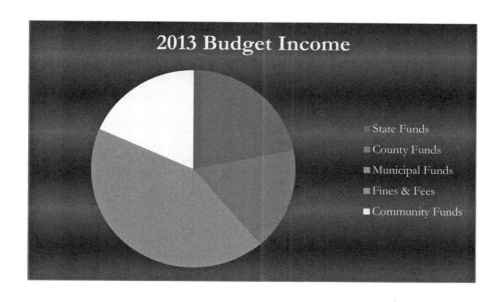

	2013	% Budget
State Funds	76,998	22%
County Funds	58,742	17%
Municipality Funds	120,266	34%
Fines & Fees	31,719	9%
Community Funds	65,296	18%

Library Board of Trustees
2013

Mark Ungemach, President—Franklin Township

Brian Gaerity, Vice President—Franklin Township

Patricia McKeon, Secretary—New London Township

Judy Porta, Treasurer—London Britain Township

Members

Anthony Caruso—London Grove Township

Eric Crist—Penn Township

Kim Fields—London Grove Township

Susan Geiger—London Grove Township

Patrick Harrison—Avondale Borough

Wanda Prosser—West Grove Borough

Suzanne Regnier—Penn Township

Cristina Reinert—West Grove Borough

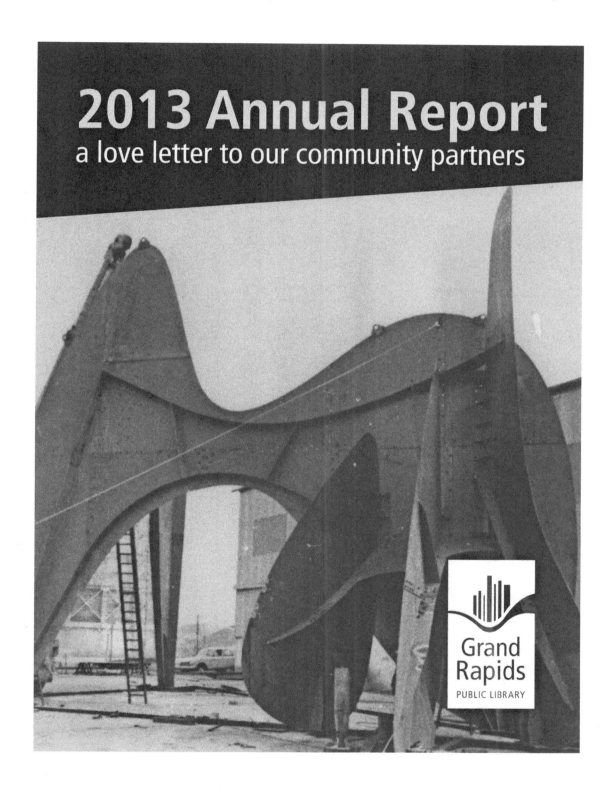

Dear Library Supporter,

Libraries are the center of our community. We shape neighborhoods, creating touch points for its citizens. People come to us for information and reflection. We provide entertainment, instruction, and connection.

The work of libraries continues to evolve and none of it would be possible without strong community partnerships. In 2013, the Grand Rapids Public Library partnered with 109 individuals, organizations, and groups to further our mission of connecting people to the transforming power of knowledge.

As library resources continue to shrink, our partnerships allow us to reach out in new and innovative ways. This year's annual report is a love letter of sorts to all of the organizations that enhance the work we do. Their commitment to our community, their openness to working together, and their limitless enthusiasm to make Grand Rapids a fun, vibrant, informed place to live and work only makes us all stronger.

Thank you.

Marcia A. Warner
Library Director

James Botts
President, Board of Library Commissioners

Construction Truck Petting Zoo

When seven municipalities provide their construction trucks for kids to climb on, sit in and honk the horn, you know they are serious about encouraging kids to **dig into reading.**

The library and the Grand Rapids Children's Museum jointly launched the Summer Reading Challenge and the Kidstruction Zone exhibit with a Construction Truck Petting Zoo. 1,500 families explored various vehicles, signed up for the Summer Reading Challenge and played at the museum.

Photo credit: Terry Johnston

Community Partners

City of East Grand Rapids
City of Grand Rapids
City of Grandville

City of Kentwood
City of Walker
City of Wyoming

Grand Rapids Children's Museum
Grand Rapids Public Library Foundation
Kent County Road Commission

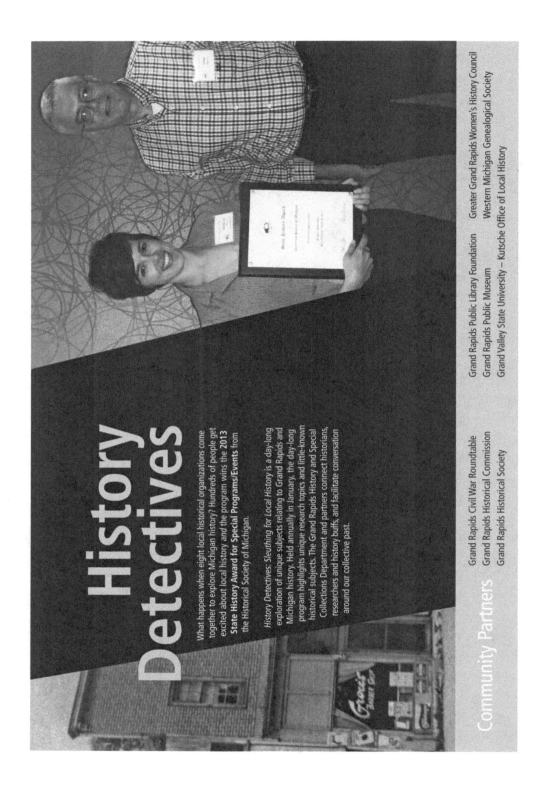

From *Crash Course in Marketing for Libraries: Second Edition* by Susan W. Alman and Sara Gillespie Swanson. Santa Barbara, CA: Libraries Unlimited. Copyright © 2015.

DigiBridge Initiative

During an assembly at Harrison Park School, a GRPL youth librarian asked how many of the students had used an eReader. One child raised his hand. **A partnership with the Grand Rapids Public Schools was born.**

The DigiBridge Initiative connects GRPS students and educators with the library's online resources and technology. Student IDs now double as library cards, allowing students easy access to our online collections. Library staff register students for full-access library cards during orientations, classroom visits, and other events. Library staff train teachers, students, and parents on a myriad of research databases to become familiar with retrieving scholarly and peer reviewed articles. Youth Services staff host a four-week Teen [Tech]Knowledgey Camp, a summer camp that teaches students how to use the library's online resources and technology in an engaging and fun environment. Students from C.A. Frost, Gerald R. Ford Academic, Harrison Park, and University Preparatory Academy have received 100 Nook eReaders loaded with grade level reading material and study questions to foster digital literacy skills. This partnership ensures our community has 21st century learners who are ready for their future careers.

Community Partners   Grand Rapids Public Library Foundation   Friends of the Grand Rapids Public Library   Grand Rapids Public Schools

Main Library Lobby Renovation

Ninety-five years after Charles R. Sligh Sr. used a $50,000 life insurance policy to create the Sligh Memorial Trust to honor his parents, his vision to create a lasting monument in Grand Rapids was reflected in the renovated lobby of the Main Library. In keeping with the vision of his contemporary, Martin Ryerson, who funded the construction of the original building, **the lobby was renovated to accommodate RFID technology** to check out material and improve customer service.

This is the second time that the Sligh Memorial Trust, which is administered by the Grand Rapids Community Foundation, provided funding to the library. The trust also supported the Furniture Design room on Level 4 of the Main Library.

Community Partners

Grand Rapids Community Foundation

Grand Rapids Public Library Foundation

Sligh Memorial Trust

Community Partners

(106) Gallery on Division
Alger Heights Business Association
Alger Heights Neighborhood Association
Area Agency on Aging of Western Michigan
ArtPrize
Baby Scholars
Bright Beginnings
Broadway Grand Rapids
Calder Investment Advisors
Calvin College—Calvin Academy for Lifelong Learning
Caregiver Resource Network
Celebration Cinema North
The Center for Michigan
Challenge Scholars
Cherry Street Health Services
Chez Olga
City of East Grand Rapids
City of Grand Rapids
City of Grand Rapids Office of Energy and Sustainability
City of Grand Rapids Parks and Recreation Department
City of Grand Rapids Mayor's 50 Program
City of Grandville
City of Kentwood
City of Walker
City of Wyoming
Cook Library Center
Dancing Goat Creamery
Duthler's Family Foods
ELO Network
Encompass

Experience Grand Rapids
Fair Housing Center of West Michigan
Family Place Libraries
First Steps
Frederick Meijer Gardens & Sculpture Park
Friends of Grand Rapids Parks
Friends of the Grand Rapids Public Library
Gerald R. Ford Presidential Museum
GR Current
Grand Rapids Area Chamber of Commerce
Grand Rapids Art Museum
Grand Rapids Audubon Club
Grand Rapids Ballet Company
Grand Rapids Bar Association
Grand Rapids Children's Museum
Grand Rapids Civic Theatre
Grand Rapids Community College
Grand Rapids Community College—Older Learner Center
Grand Rapids Community Foundation
Grand Rapids Employees Independent Union
Grand Rapids Griffins
Grand Rapids Historical Society
Grand Rapids Historical Commission
Grand Rapids Opportunities for Women
Grand Rapids Public Library Foundation
Grand Rapids Public Museum
Grand Rapids Public Schools
Grand Rapids Record & CD Show
Grand Rapids Study Club
Grand Rapids Symphony
Grand Rapids Urban League
Grand Valley State University

Grand Valley State University—Kutsche Center for Local History
Grandville Avenue Arts & Humanities
Great Start Collaborative
Greater Grand Rapids Women's History Council
Harmony Brewing Company
Institute of Museum and Library Services
John Ball Zoo
Jubilee Jobs
Kent County Road Commission
Kent District Library
Kent Intermediate School District—Kent Innovation School
Kent Regional 4 Cs
Lakeland Library Cooperative
LaughFest/Gilda's Club Grand Rapids
Library of Michigan—Michigan Center for the Book
LINC Community Revitalization Inc.
Literacy Center of West Michigan
Michigan Genealogical Council
Michigan Medicare/Medicaid Assistance Program
Michigan Small Business & Technology Development Center
Michigan State University Extension Services
Muskegon Area District Library
National Heritage Academies
Nokomis Foundation
Northern Little League
Oakdale Neighborhood Association—Boston Square Community Bikes
Opera Grand Rapids
Ottawa Hills Neighborhood Association
Parent Empowering Network

Park Place Apartments
Plachta, Murphy & Associates, P.C.
Pooh's Corner
Revue Magazine
The Right Place
Safe Kids
The Salvation Army Kroc Center
Schuler Books & Music
SCORE
Senior Coalition
Senior Leadership Grand Rapids
Shawmut Hills Garden Club
SMG/Van Andel Arena & DeVos Place
Social Security Administration
Southern Fish Fry
SpeakEZ Lounge
Specialized Language Development
St. Mary's Catholic Church
Stepping Stones Montessori
Temple Emanuel
Thomas M. Cooley Law School
Tutor Time
Uptown Kitchen
Urban Institute for Contemporary Arts
Volunteer Income Tax Assistance
West Michigan Environmental Action Council
West Michigan Hispanic Chamber of Commerce
West Michigan Research Network
West Michigan Whitecaps
Western Michigan Genealogical Society
Women's Resource Network
WZZM 13
YMCA of Greater Grand Rapids

Thanks for your dedication to our community.

2013 Board of Library Commissioners

James Botts
President

M. Jade VanderVelde
Vice President/Secretary

Anne Armstrong Cusack

William Baldridge

Ruth Lumpkins

Roger McClary

Caralee Witteveen-Lane

Marcia A. Warner
Library Director

Marla J. Ehlers
Assistant Library Director

Grand Rapids
PUBLIC LIBRARY

616.988.5400 • www.grpl.org

Grand Rapids Public Library Financial Statement

Fiscal year July 1, 2012 – June 30, 2013

Library Revenue	Operating Fund	Capital Fund	Trust Fund
Property Tax Millage	$ 8,236,191	$ 1,511,574	$ —
Penal Fines	344,974	—	—
Interest Income	35,714	12,459	1,858
Other Income	131,375	100,000	—
State Aid	136,023	—	—
Fines and Fees	210,920	—	—
Total Revenue	$ 9,095,197	$ 1,624,033	$ 1,858

Library Expenditures			
Personnel Services	$ 5,909,545	65,040	—
Building Maintenance, Utilities, Other Services	1,346,112	—	—
Collections of Books & Media	1,183,586	—	—
Capital Outlay	—	335,714	—
Other Operations	488,692	300	—
Bond Interest & Principal	—	1,816,500	—
Administrative Services	194,522	—	—
Total Expenditures	$ 9,122,457	$ 2,217,554	$ —

Library Fund Balance			
FY 2012 Surplus (Deficit)	$ (27,260)	$ (593,521)	$ 1,858
Prior Year's Balance	2,228,140	1,814,028	393,561
Ending Fund Balance	$ 2,200,880	$ 1,220,507	$ 395,419

Grand Rapids Public Library Foundation Financial Highlights

Foundation Assets

	June 30, 2013	June 30, 2012
Cash	$ 46,347	$ 55,585
Endowment Fund	2,871,478	2,472,128
Beneficial interest in Charitable Remainder Trust	88,086	81,769
Pledges receivable	106,500	212,701
Other assets	219	438
Total assets	$ 3,112,630	$ 2,822,621
Accounts and grants payable	108,471	199,053
Net assets	$ 3,004,159	$ 2,623,568

Foundation Income

Contributions and gifts	$ 294,498	$ 390,327
Investment income	79,702	118,376
Unrealized gain on investments	214,168	(134,507)
Other income	939	12,603
Total Income	$ 589,307	$ 386,799

Foundation Expenses

Grants made and granting expenses	$ 174,179	$ 423,818
Development	12,459	6,226
General and administrative	22,078	8,883
Total Expenses	$ 208,716	$ 447,927
Change in net assets	$ 380,591	$ (61,128)

2013 Board of Trustees

From *Crash Course in Marketing for Libraries: Second Edition* by Susan W. Alman and Sara Gillespie Swanson. Santa Barbara, CA: Libraries Unlimited. Copyright © 2015.

Appendix I

Sample Newsletters

Library Recognized for Award
By Leah Rudolph

The Abington Community Library in Clarks Summit received the annual Pennsylvania Library Association (PaLA) Library Support Staff Recognition Award. This award is presented to a library that has consistently encouraged and supported participation in career development activities, particularly those of PaLA, by support staff in Pennsylvania libraries. The award is presented to a library, not to a staff member.

It goes to a library that consistently:

- provides staff with opportunities to develop library skills through continuing education opportunities;
- allows staff to attend PaLA conferences and Chapter Meetings as a Support Staff member;
- provides staff with opportunities to take classes on library related activities or in areas that they can use on the job.

Staff member Sandy Longo nominated the Abington Community Library based on the strong support of the library director and trustees, who have recognized that a well-trained and highly motivated staff is essential. Staff has taken part in workshops and continuing education programs organized by the Lackawanna County Library System and relevant webinars, events organized by the Northeast Chapter of the PaLA, PaLA Annual Conference, and PaLA's Academy for Leadership Studies. In addition, staff has been encouraged to pursue degrees in Library Science, creating an educated and qualified leadership pool from which to draw upon in the future. The award was presented to the library at the PaLA Annual Conference in November, and then presented to the Board of Trustees by PaLA Northeast Chapter Chair Sheli McHugh.

Pictured: Sheli McHugh presents the award to staff member and current Master of Library and Information student Laura Gardoski and Trustee President Francis Santoriello.

Give Life During Heart Month

Every two seconds, someone needs blood. Would you help? The Abington Community Library is partnering with the Geisinger Blood Center to organize a Blood Drive. The Geisinger Blood Center processes the blood locally, so you will truly be giving back to your community in very tangible way.

On Thursday February 20 from 1-7PM, you will have the opportunity to give blood right here at the library in the Geisinger Coach. Afterwards, join us in the library for relaxation and refreshments. February is American Heart Month: what a perfect opportunity.

Interested? Be on the lookout for information from the library in January about how you can make an appointment. You must be over 17 years old to give blood.

Page 2

You "Mustache" About Winter Reading Club!
by Mary Ann McGrath

A current pop culture fad will make the Winter Reading Club more fun than ever for children who participate. From January 21 through February 28, "mustaches" will rule! Stickers, bookmarks, and even mustache finger tattoos will encourage children to spend time at the library quietly reading inside, out of the cold, and then checking out even more books to enjoy at home.

When the holidays are over and the coldest months of the year are at hand, you "mustache" for more information on how to register and take part in this fun six-week reading initiative. Recommended for youngsters from age three through 11 years old.

4th-6th Graders: Chill Out at the Library
By Nancy Burke

It might be winter, but why stay at home when there are lots of exciting events happening at the library? Whether you want to be creative at *Gingerbread House Decorating*, pop to your heart's content at *Bubble Wrap Appreciation Day*, or enjoy an interactive showing of *Despicable Me* on Valentine's Day, there's something for everyone at the library this winter.

Of course, every month you can also join us for Trivia Nights to test your knowledge, Wii Game Nights to test your gaming skills, and Yu-Gi-Oh Duels. To get information about upcoming events or register for programs, check out our website, www.lclshome.org/abington.

Also, if the due date for your end-of-semester project is fast approaching, be sure to stop by the library. With computers, Wi-Fi, and helpful librarians, you know the library is a great resource for your homework projects.

Whether you're looking for something fun to do during the long, cold months of winter, looking for facts for a research paper, or just looking for a good book, visit the library and bring a friend. You'll be glad you came!

Dorothy Boccella Holiday Marketplace
by Laura Gardoski

Dorothy Boccella Holiday Marketplace 2013 was a resounding success. A big THANK YOU goes out to all who attended, donated, or volunteered. We had hundreds of people visit our library to browse vendors' handmade items and purchase tickets for over 90 raffle baskets.

On days like our Marketplace, we see how much of a gathering place a public library can be. This building is nothing without the support of our community.

Our Holiday Marketplace was renamed this year in memory of our friend and coworker, Dorothy Boccella. Without her creativity and hard work, this successful fundraiser would not exist. Another one of her ideas was Caring Hands, a group of knitters and crotcheters who create items to donate to local non-profits. Through collaboration, people come together and accomplish worthwhile things.

So what can you do to get involved with your community? Check out your library and see! You don't have to be on staff, a Board member, or even a Friend to jump in and start something new. Bring your talent, experience, and knowledge to the library and start a club, volunteer for an event, or even run your own program.

New friendships begin here at groups that form around common interests, like the German language group Kaffeeklatsch or the Afternoon Book Club. Teens develop hobbies they love in Anime Club or in the DIY workshops. Kids come to story time when they are small and begin developing literacy skills that will last a lifetime. What do you want to do at your library? Tell us!

New Location for Young Adult Talking Books
By Sandy Longo

We've taken the young adult talking books on CD out of the adult area and created a space for them among the fiction, non-fiction, and graphic novels for teens. New and classic titles have been added that are sure to interest teens and adults that love young adult literature. Stop by and check this new area out! If there's a title that you'd like to see, please make your suggestion to staff.

"What good is the warmth of summer, without the cold of winter to give it sweetness?" John Steinbeck

Author Spotlight: Jeanne Moran

Local author Jeanne Moran has just published RISKING EXPOSURE, a novel featuring fourteen-year-old Sophie: amateur photographer and member of Hitler Youth.

Getting Started

I had published articles and short pieces in national magazines, but before *Risking Exposure* I had never attempted a novel-length work. In order to learn, I took two novel-writing courses a couple years apart. Both helped enormously at different stages of the novel's development, teaching me about research, planning, outlining, and self-editing. But like most things, I didn't really know how-to until I jumped in feet first and did it, made mistakes, and learned from them.

The Writing Process

The one step which helped me the most was writing a log-line or a pitch, sometimes called a story in a sentence. Mine was "When fourteen-year old amateur photographer and Hitler Youth member Sophie Adler contracts polio, she unintentionally starts a journey from which there is no return, one that changes her status from Nazi insider to Nazi target." I taped it over my computer and referred to when I wrote. That sentence kept me focused on my overall plan for the novel and kept my wandering imagination in check.

The Research

I traveled to Munich Germany and walked the streets where Sophie would have lived. I figured out where she would have gone to school and to church and walked through the English Garden Park where some key events in the novel take place. While there I also visited the Munich city archives, where the librarian allowed me to view 1930s city maps and photos and shared copies of them. Above all else, the trip to Munich helped me create what I hope is an authentic feel for the setting.

Want to keep reading? Check out our Library blog at http://abingtoncommunitylibrary.blogspot.com for more from Jeanne. Also, join us here at the library for an Author Talk featuring Jeanne on Tuesday, January 14 at 6:30PM. Please register.

Helping Hands Throughout the Year

Based on the success of the 2013 initiative to inviting patrons to join us in collecting for worthy local organizations, the Lackawanna County Library System has created a year-long schedule. **Drop-off of requested items may be made any time during the appropriate month at any library except Valley Community Library**. See the Library for details on specific needs as requested. Thanks!

2014 SCHEDULE:
January: Sponsored by Abington Community Library "Just Jeans in January" benefitting the St. Francis of Assisi Kitchen Clothing House
February: Sponsored by Taylor Community Library Griffin Pond Animal Shelter
March: Sponsored by Dalton Community Library Local food pantries
April: Sponsored by North Pocono Public Library Children's Advocacy Center
May: Sponsored by Carbondale Public Library Merli Veteran's Center
June: Sponsored by North Pocono Public Library Women's Resource Center
July: Sponsored by Abington Community Library Christmas in July: small gifts for the County Prison
August: Sponsored by Carbondale Public Library School supplies for local schools
September: Sponsored by Scranton Public Library, TBA
October: Sponsored by Dalton Community Library Local food pantries
November: Sponsored by Scranton Public Library, TBA
December: Sponsored by Taylor Community Library Pajama collection

---

Sweet Treats
By Sandy Longo

The Abington Community Library's Teen Leadership Committee (TLC) sells Gertrude Hawk Candy Bars: sweet treats that are perfect as stocking stuffers or valentines! You can find many varieties at the main desk of the library for just $1. What's your favorite? The proceeds benefit all that the Teen Leadership Committee hosts throughout the year, from the monthly LEGO Club to the *Junior Battle of the Books* Book Club and *All Aboard the Polar Express* program for children. New this year, they helped to support *O' the Drama: Theater Club with Rachel Strayer* in the summer. New this fall they now sponsor a new DIY (Do It Yourself Crafts) program for teens!

Please consider supporting TLC as they support many offerings for children and teens in the community.

Creativity Fuels Mind & Soul
By Sandy Longo

"There is a fountain of youth: it is your mind, your talents, the creativity you bring to your life and the lives of people you love. When you learn to tap this source, you will truly have defeated age," Sophia Loren.

Fortunately, the library happens to be a destination full of creativity. It is truly a concept we strive to put into practice daily. Where else can you find books on most any topic that you can imagine, music from all cultures and genres, instructional programs on everything from meditation, paper crafting, and how to write your own story and much more? All this is available at your library for any age, whether you're very young (Make it, Take it Craft with Mrs. McGrath), a teen (DIY), or simply young at heart (Paper Crafting with Maria Pappa, Painting on Glass with Sharon McArdle).

Make a promise to be mindful of not only bringing your children to the library for craft time but also encouraging your teens to develop a creative outlet. Fostering creativity will serve them well as they become adults and learn to navigate all that the real world has to offer. Don't forget to take the time to register yourself for a class or two. It's never too late to learn a new skill that will bring creativity back to your life and a thoughtful gift to those you love.

"You can't use up creativity. The more you use, the more you have." Maya Angelou

Friends of the Abington Community Library Membership Information

Membership runs **January—December** and includes community events **plus** early admittance to book sales!

Name_____

Address_____

_____

Phone: _____

E-mail
address:_____

Membership: $10 per person or $15 per family

Individual ___ Family ___

New ___ Renewal ___

ANNUAL FUND DRIVE UNDERWAY

Sustaining support from individuals like you enables us to offset budget pressures while ensuring that our resources and programs are specifically suited to our community's needs.

The Abington Community Library provides opportunities for patrons to read, learn, and connect with the information and people that make this Library so special. Financial support makes that happen!

The Abington Community Library:
- Serves 30,000 community members, accounting for 700,000 visits yearly;
- Provides direct support to school students that no longer benefit from full service libraries at their schools;
- Runs dozens of children and teen programs designed to encourage a life-long love of reading and foster community service;
- Serves as the meeting place for a diverse range of interests, such as book groups, game clubs, knitting circles, and art enthusiasts;
- Hosts numerous information and training sessions on topics such as career planning, tax preparation, financial planning, and more.

Our Annual Fund Drive runs now through the end of the year. By making a tax-deductible contribution via check or through PayPal on our website, you'll be supporting a vibrant, growing center of activity in this community. Thank you in advance for your continued support.

NON-FICTION FOR EMERGENT READERS
By Mary Ann McGrath

There is a growing emphasis on non-fiction books these days, linked to Common Core Standards and a changing approach to how children can best achieve success in school, college and career. Parents may be interested to know that their preschoolers and emergent readers will find a growing collection of non-fiction just for them in the Children's Room.

To make it more feasible for youngsters to find books that interest them specifically, the staff has arranged them in groups under topics. Some of the topics, chosen for high interest among this age group, include: Farm Animals, Pets, Wild Animals, Dinosaurs, Birds, Science, Solar System, Holidays, Vehicles, Community Helpers, and Sports. Most are illustrated with photos and include a list of vocabulary words.

PROGRAMS FOR ALL AGES

Most programs will be conducted at the Library unless otherwise noted. Register by visiting the Library or by calling 570.587.3440. Check the Library or website for programs added after this newsletter has gone to print. These programs/displays/events are sponsored by the Abington Community Library as part of the *PA Forward* initiative promoting the value of libraries in the 21st Century.

December 2013

All Month **STORY TIMES FOR CHILDREN** Tuesday, December 3: 10:30 am and 1:30 pm for 3 though 5 year olds; Thursday December 5: 10:30 am for 2 & 3 year olds; Alternate Fridays December 6: 10:30 am for 1 through 3 year olds (Story & Playtime). Pre-registration is requested!

December 1 through December 29 **ST. JOSEPH'S SOCK COLLECTION** Donations of young children's socks may be hung on the Sock Tree in the library's Children's Room for the benefit of St. Joseph's Center's Mother/Infant Pantry. All ages.

Every Tuesday (ongoing program) **BRIDGE GROUP** 1 to 3 PM New members always welcome for this social bridge group. Adults.

Every Tuesday (ongoing program) **MAH JONGG** 1 to 3 PM Join our group of National Mah Jongg League, Inc. players. No experience necessary. Adults.

Every Monday (ongoing program) **CARING HANDS GROUP** 1 PM Do you knit or crochet? Consider joining this new group whose members meet to create items which are needed by local non-profit agencies. Grade 7–Adults.

Every other Monday (Dec. 2, 16, & 30) **KNITTING GROUP** 6:30 to 7:30 PM Bring your current project and knit with others. Adults.

Every Wednesday (ongoing program) **BRIDGE GROUP** 10 AM to 12 Noon New members always welcome for this social bridge group. Adults.

Every Wednesday (ongoing program) **FAMILIES HELPING FAMILIES** 7 to 8:30 PM Facilitators provide an educational series and support group for teens and their families affected by substance abuse. Co-sponsored by the Clear Brook Foundation. Adults.

Every Thursday (ongoing program) **SCRABBLE** 1 PM Join our enthusiastic group of Scrabble players for a fun game! No registration necessary. Adults.

Sunday, Dec. 1 **BARRYMORE'S GHOST DRAMATIC READING** 3 to 4 PM Experience a reading of the play "Barrymore's Ghost," performed by actor Robert Hughes. Note: This play contains adult language. Adults.

Thursday, Dec. 5 **EATING WELL (DESPITE THE HOLIDAYS!)** 6:30 to 7:30 PM Join Stefanie M. Evanko, registered dietician from Geisinger Health Plan for a Family Nutrition Program. She will be providing a variety of information to help you incorporate healthy meal choices at home including healthy eating tips, tips for adding fruits and vegetables in your child's diet, recipes, and more! Adults.

Friday, Dec. 6, 13, 20, and 27 **ANIME CLUB** 4 to 6 PM Join us for some ANIMated fun! Bring along a friend. Grades 7–12.

Saturday, Dec. 7 **TEEN PEER WRITING GROUP** 11:30 AM to 12:30 PM Many authors suggest that if you want to be a writer, you must write, every day. Come and write, share and inspire . . . yourself and others. Please bring your own writing materials. Grades 7–12.

Saturday, Dec. 7 **HOLIDAY ELF STORY TIME** 11 AM to noon Special guest Gretchen Kohut will portray an Elf as she entertains children and adults with holiday stories. Bring a camera to record the event. Families with children of all ages.

Saturday, Dec. 7 **YU-GI-Oh DUEL!** 1 to 3 PM Unleash some of your strongest monsters in our duel. Bring along your Yu-Gi-Oh cards and a friend! Sponsored by the Teen Leadership Committee. Grades 4–12.

Sunday, Dec. 8 **A CHILD'S CHRISTMAS IN WALES** 3 to 3:45 PM Experience a reading of A CHILD'S CHRISTMAS IN WALES, by Dylan Thomas and performed by actor Robert Hughes. It will be a nostalgic look back at a time when life was simpler. All ages.

Monday, Dec. 9 **SIGNING SANTA** 6 to 7 PM Come and meet our Signing Santa for a story, hot chocolate, photo opportunities, and fun! Ages Birth—7. Siblings welcome!

Tuesday, Dec. 10 **MYSTERY & DETECTIVES BOOK CLUB** 7 to 8:30 PM Read any Detective Maigret novel by Georges Simenon. Adults.

Thursday, Dec. 12 **KAFFEEKLATSCH** 7 PM All are invited to join this German language conversation group. Practice speaking and listening; all levels wilkommen! Adults.

Friday, Dec. 13 **GAME NIGHT WITH Wii** 6:30 to 8 PM Join us for some OVERSIZED fun! Bring along a friend. Grades 4–6.

Sunday, Dec. 15 **ALL ABOARD THE POLAR EXPRESS** 6 PM Join us for our traditional event with a special reading of Chris Van Allsburg's classic THE POLAR EXPRESS. Hot chocolate will be served. We invite you to wear your pajamas! Sponsored by Abington Community Library Teen Leadership Committee. SNOW DATE: SUNDAY, DECEMBER 22, 6 PM. Children.

Tuesday, Dec. 17 **MAKE-IT, TAKE-IT CRAFT TIME** 3 PM TO 5 PM Make construction paper TRAINS for colorful holiday decorations.

Drop in any time during the hours listed. Everything will be provided. Ages 3–10.

Tuesday, Dec. 17 **HOOKED ON CROCHET** 6:30—8:30 PM Bring your current project to this open forum of crocheters; share a few crocheting tips or learn a few new ones. Grades 7–Adult.

Wednesday, Dec. 18 **AFTERNOON BOOK CLUB** 2 to 3 PM THE FIVE PEOPLE YOU MEET IN HEAVEN by Mitch Albom. Adults.

Thursday, Dec. 19 **AFTER-SCHOOL PROGRAM** 4 to 4:45 PM Book a Trip to GERMANY. Hear the history of the Christmas tree and listen to a story about the origin of tinsel. Facts, folklore & fun! Ages 7–10.

Thursday, Dec. 19 **AFTER SCHOOL DIY (DO IT YOURSELF) FOR TEENS** 4 to 5:30 PM Project TBD. All materials will be supplied. Sponsored by Abington Community Library Teen Leadership Committee. Grades 7–12.

Thursday, Dec. 19 **PAPER CRAFTING WITH MARIA PAPPA** 6 to 8 PM Project TBD. Materials Cost: $10, paid to the instructor the day of the class. Adults.

Friday, Dec. 20 **SMARTY-PANTS TRIVIA NIGHT** 6:30 to 7:30 PM Be competitive, challenge yourself, and hang out with friends at this Trivia Night! Enjoy a game of Jeopardy, plus more trivia. Bring your friends and play to win prizes! Grades 4–6.

Saturday, Dec. 21 **GINGERBREAD HOUSE DECORATING** 10 to 11 AM Decorate a graham cracker house and make homemade poppers to take home for the holidays! Grades 4–6.

Tuesday, Dec. 24 **CLOSED FOR CHRISTMAS EVE** Library is closed but we're open 24/7 at www.lclshome.org/abington.

Wednesday, Dec. 25 **CLOSED FOR CHRISTMAS DAY** Library is closed but we're open 24/7 at www.lclshome.org/abington.

Thursday, Dec. 26 **LA CHIACCHIERATA: ITALIAN DISCUSSION GROUP** 7 PM All are invited to join our self-guided Friends of the Italian Language conversation group. Tap into the Italian language treasure and culture by practicing the language with others. All levels of language experience welcome. No registration required. For Grades 10/11–Adult.

Friday, Dec. 27 **FOURTH FRIDAYS ACOUSTIC MUSIC** 6:30 to 8:30 PM Bring your own acoustic instrument and join in on the jammin'. All ages.

Tuesday, Dec. 31 **NEARLY NEW YEAR'S EVE** 11 AM to 12 PM Celebrate the start of 2014 with games, food, and fun! Grades 4–6.

Tuesday, Dec. 31 **EARLY CLOSING AT 5 PM FOR NEW YEAR'S EVE** Library is closed but we're open 24/7 at www.lclshome.org/abington.

January 2014

All Month **STORY TIMES FOR CHILDREN** Tuesday January 14, 21, & 28 @ 10:30 am and 1:30 pm for ages 3 through 5 year olds; Thursday January 16, 23, & 30 @ 10:30 am for 2 & 3 year olds; Friday January 10 & 14 @ 10:30 am for 1 through 3 year olds (Story and Playtime). Pre-registration is requested!

From *Crash Course in Marketing for Libraries: Second Edition* by Susan W. Alman and Sara Gillespie Swanson. Santa Barbara, CA: Libraries Unlimited. Copyright © 2015.

Every Monday (ongoing program) **CARING HANDS GROUP** 1 PM Do you knit or crochet? Consider joining this new group whose members meet to create items which are needed by local non-profit agencies. Grade 7–Adults.

Every Tuesday (ongoing program) **BRIDGE GROUP** 1 to 3 PM New members always welcome for this social bridge group. Adults.

Every Tuesday (ongoing program) **MAH JONGG** 1 to 3 PM Join our group of National Mah Jongg League, Inc. players. No experience necessary. Adults.

Every Wednesday (ongoing program) **BRIDGE GROUP** 10 AM to 12 Noon New members always welcome for this social bridge group. Adults.

Every Wednesday (ongoing program) **FAMILIES HELPING FAMILIES** 7 to 8:30 PM Facilitators provide an educational series and support group for teens and their families affected by substance abuse. Co-sponsored by the Clear Brook Foundation. Adults.

Every Thursday (ongoing program) **SCRABBLE** 1 PM Join our enthusiastic group of Scrabble players for a fun game! No registration necessary. Adults.

Every Friday (ongoing program) **ANIME CLUB** 4 to 6 PM Join us for some ANIMated fun! Bring along a friend. Grades 7—12

Wednesday, Jan. 1 **CLOSED FOR NEW YEAR'S DAY** Library is closed but we're open 24/7 at www.lclshome.org/abington.

Friday, Jan. 3 **GAME NIGHT WITH Wii** 6:30 to 8 PM Join us for OVERSIZED fun! Bring along a friend. Grades 4–6 PM

Thursday, Jan. 9 **QUILTING** 6 to 8 PM Bring your current project. Adults.

Monday, Jan. 13 **WRITING YOUR MEMOIR** 6 to 8 PM Learn how to write your story in this 10-week series taught by Carol Brennan King: Jan. 13, 27; Feb. 3, 10, 24; March 3, 10, 17, 24, 31. Adults.

Tuesday, Jan. 14 **MAKE-IT, TAKE-IT CRAFT TIME** 3 to 5 PM Make WINTER-themed crafts. Drop in any time during the hours listed. Everything will be provided. Ages 3–10.

Tuesday, Jan. 14 **AUTHOR TALK: JEANNE MORAN** 6:30 to 8 PM Join local author Jeanne Moran as she shares the challenges and triumphs of creating the backdrop for her historical fiction novel RISKING EXPOSURE set in Nazi Germany. From research of the historical timeline to decisions on setting, she'll review her decision-making in words and pictures. Books will be available for purchase and signing.

Grade 7-Adult.

Thursday, Jan. 16 **YOUR MOBILE DEVICE: THE BASICS** 10:30 to 11:30AM Attend a workshop on using your new mobile device.

Learn how to navigate, install apps, and get library ebooks. Featuring: Kindle & Windows. Adults.

Thursday, Jan. 16 **WRITING YOUR MEMOIR PART** 2 2 to 4 PM Learn how to write your story in this 10-week series taught by Carol Brennan King: Jan. 16, 23, 30; Feb. 6, 13, 20, 27; March 6, 13, 20. This is a continuation of the fall workshops, but newcomers are welcome. Adults.

Thursday, Jan. 16 **DIY FOR TEENS** 4 PM to 5:30 PM Project: TBD. All materials will be supplied. Sponsored by Abington Community Library Teen Leadership Committee. Teens.

Thursday, Jan. 16 **PAPER CRAFTING WITH MARIA PAPPA** 6 PM Project: TBD. All materials will be supplied. Sponsored by Abington Community Library Teen Leadership Committee. Adults.

Friday, Jan. 17 **SMARTY-PANTS TRIVIA NIGHT** 6:30 to 7:30 PM Be competitive, challenge yourself, and hang out with friends at this Trivia Night! Enjoy a game of Jeopardy, plus more trivia. Bring your friends and play to win prizes! Grades 4–6.

Monday, Jan. 20 **CLOSED FOR MARTIN LUTHER KING DAY** Library is closed but we're open 24/7 at www.lclshome.org/abington.

Thursday, Jan. 23 **YOUR MOBILE DEVICE: THE BASICS** 10:30 11:30 AM Attend a workshop on using your new mobile device. Learn how to navigate, install apps, and get library ebooks. Featuring: Android & iPad. Adults.

Thursday, Jan. 23 **WRITING YOUR MEMOIR PART** 2 2 to 4 PM Learn how to write your story in this 10-week series taught by Carol Brennan King: Jan. 16, 23, 30; Feb. 6, 13, 20, 27; March 6, 13, 20. This is a continuation of the fall workshops, but newcomers are welcome. Adults.

Thursday, Jan. 23 **QUILTING** 6 PM Bring your current project. Adults.

Friday, Jan. 24 **STORY TIME TEENS** 6:30 to 7:30 PM Join us for an Interactive Evening Story Time! Sponsored by the Teen Leadership Committee. Presented by Story Time Teens. THEME: Being Grumpy. Ages 3–6. Siblings welcome!

Saturday, Jan. 25 **CHAINMAIL BRACELET WITH LAURA DONATH** 2 to 4 PM Create a unique chainmail bracelet with Laura Donath. A Materials Fee in the amount of TBD paid to the instructor at the beginning of class. Adults.

Monday, Jan. 27 **WRITING YOUR MEMOIR** 6 to 8 PM Learn how to write your story in this 10-week series taught by Carol Brennan King: Jan. 13, 27; Feb. 3, 10, 24; March 3, 10, 17, 24, 31. Adults.

Wednesday, Jan. 29 **NATIONAL PUZZLE DAY** Join us for a puzzle exchange, or piece one together here. All ages.

Thursday, Jan. 30 **WRITING YOUR MEMOIR PART 2** 2 to 4 PM Learn how to write your story in this 10-week series taught by Carol Brennan King: Jan. 16, 23, 30; Feb. 6, 13, 20, 27; March 6, 13, 20. This is a continuation of the fall workshops, but newcomers are welcome. Adults.

Friday, Jan. 31 **BUBBLE WRAP APPRECIATION** DAY 6:30 to 7:30 PM Celebrate with games, crafts and bubble wrap fun! Grades 4–6.

February 2014

All Month **STORY TIMES FOR CHILDREN** Tuesday, February 4 & 11 @ 10:30 am and 1:30 pm for ages 3 through 5 year olds; Thursday February 6 & 13 @ 10:30 am for 2 & 3 year olds; Friday, February 7 & 21 @ 10:30 am for 1 through 3 year olds (Story and Playtime).

Pre-registration is requested!

February 7 through February 28 **GRIFFIN POND ANIMAL SHELTER COLLECTION** Drop off donated pet supplies to the collection barrel. All ages.

Every Monday (ongoing program) **CARING HANDS GROUP** 1 PM Do you knit or crochet? Consider joining this new group whose members meet to create items which are needed by local non-profit agencies. Grade 7–Adults.

Every Tuesday (ongoing program) **BRIDGE GROUP** 1 to 3 PM New members always welcome for this social bridge group. Adults.

Every Tuesday (ongoing program) **MAH JONGG** 1 to 3 PM Join our group of National Mah Jongg League, Inc. players. No experience necessary. Adults.

Every Wednesday (ongoing program) **BRIDGE GROUP** 10 AM to 12 Noon New members always welcome for this social bridge group. Adults.

Every Wednesday (ongoing program) **FAMILIES HELPING FAMILIES** 7 to 8:30 PM Facilitators provide an educational series and support group for teens and their families affected by substance abuse. Co-sponsored by the Clear Brook Foundation. Adults.

Every Thursday (ongoing program) **SCRABBLE** 1 PM Join our enthusiastic group of Scrabble players for a fun game! No registration necessary. Adults.

Every Friday (ongoing program) **ANIME CLUB** 4 to 6 PM Join us for some ANIMated fun! Bring along a friend. Grades 7–12.

Monday, Feb. 3 **WRITING YOUR MEMOIR** 6 to 8 PM Learn how to write your story in this 10-week series taught by Carol Brennan King: Jan. 13, 27; Feb. 3, 10, 24; March 3, 10, 17, 24, 31. Adults.

Thursday, Feb. 6 **WRITING YOUR MEMOIR PART 2** 2 to 4 PM Learn how to write your story in this 10-week series taught by Carol Brennan King: Jan. 16, 23, 30; Feb. 6, 13, 20, 27; March 6, 13, 20. This is a continuation of the fall workshops, but newcomers are welcome. Adults.

Friday, Feb. 7 **GAME NIGHT WITH Wii** 6:30 to 8 PM Join us for some OVERSIZED fun! Bring along a friend. Grades 4–6.

Monday, Feb. 10 **MAKE-IT, TAKE-IT CRAFT TIME** 3 to 5 PM Make VALENTINES. Drop in any time during the hours listed. Everything will be provided. Ages 3–10.

Monday, Feb. 10 **WRITING YOUR MEMOIR** 6 to 8 PM Learn how to write your story in this 10-week series taught by Carol Brennan King: Jan. 13, 27; Feb. 3, 10, 24; March 3, 10, 17, 24, 31. Adults.

From *Crash Course in Marketing for Libraries: Second Edition* by Susan W. Alman and Sara Gillespie Swanson. Santa Barbara, CA: Libraries Unlimited. Copyright © 2015.

Thursday, Feb. 13 **WRITING YOUR MEMOIR PART 2** 2 to 4 PM Learn how to write your story in this 10-week series taught by Carol Brennan King: Jan. 16, 23, 30; Feb. 6, 13, 20, 27; March 6, 13, 20. This is a continuation of the fall workshops, but newcomers are welcome.

Thursday, Feb. 13 **QUILTING** 6 to 8 PM Bring your current project. Adults.

Friday Feb. 14 **DESPICABLE ME INTERACTIVE MOVIE** 6:30 to 8:30 PM Sing, play, shout along with the movie! Props and light refreshments will be served. Grades 4–6.

Monday, Feb. 17 **CLOSED FOR PRESIDENTS DAY** Library is closed but we're open 24/7 at www.lclshome.org/abington.

Thursday, Feb. 20 **GEISINGER BLOOD CENTER DRIVE** 1 to 7 PM Schedule your appointment at the library and give blood! Adults.

Thursday, Feb. 20 **WRITING YOUR MEMOIR PART 2** 2 to 4 PM Learn how to write your story in this 10-week series taught by Carol Brennan King: Jan. 16, 23, 30; Feb. 6, 13, 20, 27; March 6, 13, 20. This is a continuation of the fall workshops, but newcomers are welcome. Adults.

Thursday, Feb. 20 **DIY FOR TEENS** 4 PM to 5:30 PM Project: TBD. All materials will be supplied. Sponsored by Abington Community Library Teen Leadership Committee. Teens.

Thursday, Feb. 20 **PAPER CRAFTING WITH MARIA PAPPA** 6 PM Project: TBD. Adults.

Friday, Feb. 21 **SMARTY-PANTS TRIVIA NIGHT** 6:30 to 7:30 PM Be competitive, challenge yourself, and hang out with friends at this Trivia Night! Enjoy a game of Jeopardy, plus more trivia. Bring your friends and play to win prizes! Grades 4–6.

Monday, Feb. 24 **WRITING YOUR MEMOIR** 6 to 8 PM Learn how to write your story in this 10-week series taught by Carol Brennan King: Jan. 13, 27; Feb. 3, 10, 24; March 3, 10, 17, 24, 31. Adults.

Thursday, Feb. 27 **WRITING YOUR MEMOIR PART 2** 2 to 4 PM Learn how to write your story in this 10-week series taught by Carol Brennan King: Jan. 16, 23, 30; Feb. 6, 13, 20, 27; March 6, 13, 20. This is a continuation of the fall workshops, but newcomers are welcome. Adults.

Thursday, Feb. 27 **QUILTING** 6 to 8 PM Bring your current project. Adults.

Friday, Feb. 28 **STORY TIME TEENS** 6:30 to 7:30 PM Join us for an Interactive Evening Story Time! Sponsored by the Teen Leadership Committee. Presented by Story Time Teens. THEME: Baking/Cooking. Ages 3–6. Siblings welcome!

1200 West Grove St.
Clarks Summit, PA 18411

Phone: 570.587.3440

Use our website to check on
Holiday or snow closings:
www.lclshome.org/Abington

For upcoming programs,
click on "Library Events."

Become a member of our
Friends! Ask any staff
member for an application
or visit our website
www.lclshome.org/abington.

Regular Library Hours

Monday-Friday 9 am – 9 pm
Saturday   9 am – 5 pm
Sunday   2 pm – 5 pm

Abington Community Library Honorariums and Memorials

Recent contributions to the Library are greatly appreciated
and include:

MEMORIALS

Joan Namey
In memory of Matthew Mackie,
Gretchen and Richard Miller
donated a book display and
Kay White donated ten chairs
for the staff break room.

Abington Community Library Mission Statement

The Abington Community Library's mission is to facilitate lifelong learning, provide for leisure-time
interests, support student research, and encourage children, teens, and adults to read.
Adopted August 2008

Abington Community Library
1200 West Grove St.
Clarks Summit, PA 18411-9501

MT. LEBANON PUBLIC LIBRARY : **more friends**

Friends of the Mt. Lebanon Library Newsletter

February 2014 ● Volume XL ● Issue 6

Universal Class at your fingertips!

Learn something new this month by checking out *Universal Class*.

Visit the library's web site http://www.mtlebanonlibrary.org/reference/databases-topics#Education and click on *Universal Class* where you can choose from more than 500 non-credit continuing education courses for personal enrichment on many subjects, such as Accounting, Cooking, Crafts & Hobbies, Small Business, Spiritual Studies, Test Preparation, and Yoga. Access to your course is available 24/7 via the Internet—at the library or at home. Attend class and do assignments on your own schedule. Each course has a real instructor with whom you may communicate using email. Register and learn something new today! *This database is funded by Mt. Lebanon Public Library.*

The Book Cellar Needs Non-Fiction

The Book Cellar had a booming holiday season! We offer a rousing thanks to all our shoppers. But with the good sometimes comes the bad, and for the shop that is a low non-fiction inventory level. We especially need books on the subjects of art, cooking, crafts, Civil War history, and travel, along with other non-fiction titles.

If you are planning on making space in your library for newer titles, please consider donating your unwanted books, DVDs, CDs, baubles, and other resale items to the library's Book Cellar.

Donations are accepted anytime during normal library hours. The cart is located at the end of the lower-level hallway facing Castle Shannon Blvd. Thank you!

Inside this issue

To register for any programs or for more information, call the library at 412-531-1912 or email events@ mtlebanonlibrary.org.

Keep up with events via mtlebanonlibrary.org, **Facebook and Twitter!**

Green Programs Coming Up...

VEGETABLE GARDENING AND SEED SHARING EVENT
Saturday, February 22, 10:00am

New vegetable seeds will be divided amongst and by the participants. Thirty kinds of vegetables were selected! The number of seeds of each type varies, e.g. only three melon seeds (because that is all you need!) but 40 lettuce seeds (because you'll need that many!). Participants share the cost and the work of dividing up the seeds. Also please plan to share your stories of lessons you have learned – good and bad – about raising vegetables. Contact Mary Beth at mbthakar@yahoo.com or 412-736-8216 to secure a spot or ask for additional information. Come early on seed "sharing" day to be sure to keep your spot, paying at the door ($10 per person – for hundreds of seeds – a really great deal!). Seeds were chosen (mostly organic and non-GMO) from the Fedco Seed catalog, with the view of trying new and different varieties, but "sharing" the seeds keeps costs low. Space is limited to 20 individuals, so register early – and come on time!

LANDSCAPE DESIGN COURSE
Monday, February 24, 6:00pm (and March 3 and 10)

Claire Schuchman will teach a three-week course geared to the novice. It will use the concepts of sustainable design like "right plant/right place"; shading out weeds with ground covers; use of hardy native plants; and installing rain barrels or permeable pavement. Please bring graph paper, pencils, ruler, package of different colored pencils, a few stakes and some 18"- 24" tracing paper. Students will benefit from having a plot plan or a survey of their property if available and pictures of gardens they like. Claire Schuchman is a local landscape designer, Phipps Master Gardener, and frequent contributor to the Mt Lebanon Magazine. The program is presented in cooperation with the Mt. Lebanon Garden Tour Committee.

THE BOOK CELLAR
Used Bookstore
Lower level of the library

Hours:

Monday 10-8
Tuesday 10-8
Wednesday 10-8
Thursday 10-8
Friday & Saturday 10-4
Sunday closed

All proceeds go to the library.

Be a Volunteer Literacy Tutor

Speaking and understanding English are necessary survival skills for foreign-born adults living in the U.S. You can help these adults to improve their English skills and learn about American customs by becoming a volunteer tutor for Greater Pittsburgh Literacy Council.

Call Jessamine at 412-393-7600 or Peggi at 412-531-3004 for more information.

From *Crash Course in Marketing for Libraries: Second Edition* by Susan W. Alman and Sara Gillespie Swanson. Santa Barbara, CA: Libraries Unlimited. Copyright © 2015.

2 **FROM THE DIRECTOR**

*Tribute to Maite Schmidt
on the Occasion of Her Retirement*

February 2014

A public library is only as good as its staff. The community benefits best from excellent collections, creative programs, and special services when staff effectively coordinates those activities and serves as a conduit to residents. Library Assistant Maite Schmidt exemplifies the very best. She welcomes, encourages, and nurtures those who pass through the library's doors—patrons and staff alike. With unparalleled skill and devotion, Maite has provided stellar service to the library for the past 33 years, and will retire on February 8 to move to rural Massachusetts near her daughter Amy (a former page at our library!), son-in-law, and two grandchildren.

Although Maite studied at the Institute of Radio Technology in her native Germany, she found her true calling in our public library, first as a volunteer starting in 1981 and then as a part-time member of the staff in 1983. She was promoted to full-time library assistant in 1986. Maite has served the library and our community with distinction, setting high standards and helping staff and volunteers achieve them. She has been a peerless staff and volunteer trainer and a generous mentor to many. Her insights into public service and her ideas for streamlining and serving the public amid countless changes over the decades have made a big difference in how we do our work. Her organizational skills are matchless.

No job is ever too big or too small for Maite—she delves into everything with her signature industry and dedication. Maite has made significant contributions: everything from periodicals management and new staff and volunteer training to finding books for patrons and making all the "Library closed for the holiday" signs for our doors. For the last 20 years or so, Maite even volunteered to empty our book return boxes every single Sunday and holiday. She also volunteered to translate German documents for library patrons all over the county, particularly Fractur which few can do.

Her contributions have extended well beyond library work: she is an accomplished painter, craftswoman, knitter, cook and baker, too, and she is always willing to share her knowledge with others. Maite is a patient, effective teacher. She is wonderful with children when they receive their first library cards. And Maite enthusiastically helps with every creative program and fundraising activity at the library.

We are so glad that Maite chose to devote her career to this library she loves. We will miss her prodigious talents, creative thinking, kind and gracious manner, cheerfulness, keen sense of humor, and generosity of spirit. We know that everyone will join us in wishing Maite the very best as she embarks on this next chapter of her life.

Ein herzliches Dankeschön, Maite!

Cynthia K. Richey

KIDS **3**

CHILDREN'S STORYTIMES

Bonjour Les Amis
Mondays, February 3, 10, 17, and 24
10:30am
Stories and fun in French for children ages 2 - 5 and their parents. Please pre-register.

Hola Ninos
Mondays, February 3, 10, 17, and 24, 1:15pm
Stories and fun in Spanish for kids ages 3 - 6 and their parents.

Wild About Books - Storytime Fun!
Tuesdays, February 4, 11, 18, and 25, 10:00am
Storytime fun for children ages 4 - 6.

Book Babies
Wednesdays, February 5, 12, 19, and 26
9:30am, 10:15am, 11:00am
Stories, songs and rhymes for children ages birth - 2 years with an adult.

Storytime for 2s & 3s
Thursdays, February 6, 13, 20, and 27
9:30am, 10:15am, 11:00am
Stories, songs, and rhymes for children ages 2 - 3 with an adult.

Sensory Storytime
Friday, February 14, 10:00am
Stories, movement, and sensory play activities for children ages 3 - 5 and a caregiver. A small group storytime with adaptations. Great for children on the autism spectrum. Space is limited; please pre-register.

Pajama Storytime
Tuesday, February 18, 6:30pm
An evening storytime for children ages 3 - 7 and their families. Stories, songs, rhymes and fun activities.

OPEN ART STUDIO SATURDAYS!
Saturday, February 1, 9:30am - 4:30pm

Stop by the children's library anytime today and make a simple art project to take home!

SUNDAY FUNDAYS
Sundays, February 2, 9, 16, and 23
1:30pm

Activities for the whole family!

TUESDAY CRAFTERNOON
Tuesdays, February 4, 11, 18, and 25
4:00pm

Join in some craft fun after school, for kids in grades 1 - 3.

CHESS CLUB
Tuesday, February 4, 6:30pm

Fun with chess for kids in kindergarten - grade 7.

EZ MATH WORKSHOP FOR 3RD-6TH GRADERS
Wednesdays, February 5, 12, 19, and 26
6:00pm

This new EZ Math workshop is a series of seven free classes, open to any student in grades 3 - 6. The goal of the volunteer instructors for this group, scientists Lei Hong and Jie Feng, is to help youngsters develop a deep appreciation and understanding of math skills in a short time. The children are encouraged to engage in logical reasoning and critical thinking. Mr. Hong and Mr. Feng will demonstrate problem-solving techniques that will help make math fun for children. There is no registration necessary to participate, but students should come to each session with paper and pencils.

TAIL WAGGING TUTORS
Thursday, February 6, 7:00pm

Children can read aloud to a furry friend! Dog listeners are trained by Therapy Dogs International. Registration is required.

LITTLE ACHIEVERS' WEE PLAY GROUP
Friday, February 7, 10:30am

All children 18 months to 3 years of age are invited to join early childhood professionals from ACHIEVA Support Early Intervention Program at a monthly one-hour playgroup. Every child will be encouraged to play at his/her developmental level. Parents and caregivers must stay with the children. Register online at http://www.achieva.info (Early Intervention tab [top left], click on ACHIEVA's Inclusive Community Playgroup).

CHESS TOURNAMENT
Saturday, February 8
1:00pm – 5:00pm

It's the 41st annual Library Chess Tournament for children in grades K – 8! Players MUST pre-register by calling 412-531-1912, ext. 4. Two divisions: grades K – 4 and grades 5 – 8.

LEGO CLUB
Wednesday, February 26, 4:00pm

Have fun building things with Legos! Kids must pre-register (the club is for ages 7 - 12).

Saturday, Feb. 1   9:30 AM–4:30 PM **Open Art Studio Saturdays!**   See p. 3
1:00 PM **South Hills Scrabble Club**   See p. 6
6:00 PM **Brews for a Chili Night IV**   See p. 1

Sunday, February 2 1:30 PM **Sunday Fundays**   See p. 3

Monday, February 3 10:00 AM **Morning Spanish Literature & Conversation Group**   Speak and read in Spanish on a variety of topics; all abilities welcome!
10:30 AM **Bonjour Les Amis**   See p. 3
10:30 AM **Shakespeare Readers**   See p. 8
12:30 PM **Readers' Theater Rehearsal**
1:15 PM **Hola Ninos!**   See p. 3
7:00 PM **Good Friends: Comfort Food for the Soul**   See p. 6
7:00 PM **Slovak Heritage**   "Egg Decorating Eggstravaganza": Mike Yanchak will show/demonstrate styles of decorated eggs (pisanki).
7:30 PM **Sahaja Meditation**   See p. 6

Tuesday, Feb. 4   10:00 AM **Wild About Books—Storytime Fun!**   See p. 3
10:00 AM **Mt. Lebanon Conversation Salon**   Join friends and neighbors in talking about current events and issues touching all our lives.
11:00 AM **English Learners' Book Club**   See p. 8
4:00 PM **Tuesday Crafternoon**   See p. 3
6:30 PM **Chess Club**   See p. 3
7:00 PM **Myths and Facts about Hospice Care**   See p. 6

Wednesday, Feb. 5 9:30, 10:15, 11:00 AM **Book Babies**   See p. 3
10:00 AM **English Conversation Class**   Practice your English in an informal setting. Please register by emailing pkelley@gplc.org.
10:00 AM **Francophone Literature & Culture**   Read and discuss in French the modern and classical writers of the Francophone world.
12:30 PM **Readers' Theater Rehearsal**
2:00 PM **Creative Connections**   See p. 6
3:30 PM **Wii Wednesdays**   See p. 6
6:00 PM **EZ Math Workshop for 3rd-6th Graders**   See p. 3
6:30 PM **Crazy for Comics!**   See p. 8
7:00 PM **Independent Nights: a Library Film Series**   See p. 6
7:30 PM **Yoga for You**   See p. 7

Thursday, Feb. 6   9:15 AM **American History Book Discussion Group**   See p. 8
9:30, 10:15, 11:00 AM **Storytime for 2s & 3s**   See p. 3
10:00 AM **Advanced Italian Conversation**   Join a lively and fun group reading and speaking the Italian language!
12:30 PM **League of Women Voters Lunchtime Series**   See p. 7
3:15 PM **Otaku Lebo**   See p. 6
7:00 PM **Tail Wagging Tutors**   See p. 3
7:00 PM **Conversational Chinese and Chinese Culture**   Practice conversational Chinese and explore the culture. All levels welcome.
7:15 PM **South Hills Flute Choir**   Flute players with at least three years of playing experience (all ages welcome) are invited to practice.

Friday, February 7 10:30 AM **Little Achievers' Wee Play group**   See p. 3
12:30 PM **Readers' Theater Rehearsal**

Saturday, Feb. 8   1:00 PM **South Hills Scrabble Club**   See p. 6
1:00 PM–5:00 PM **Kids Chess Tournament**   See p. 3

Sunday, February 9 1:30 PM **Sunday Fundays**   See p. 3

Monday, Feb. 10   10:00 AM **Morning Spanish Literature & Conversation Group**   Speak and read in Spanish on a variety of topics every week.
10:30 AM **Bonjour Les Amis**   See p. 3
10:30 AM **Morning Book Discussion Group**   See p. 8
12:30 PM **Readers' Theater Rehearsal**
1:15 PM **Hola Ninos!**   See p. 3
6:30 PM **American Girl Book Club**   See p. 8

From *Crash Course in Marketing for Libraries: Second Edition* by Susan W. Alman and Sara Gillespie Swanson. Santa Barbara, CA: Libraries Unlimited. Copyright © 2015.

	7:30 PM Sahaja Meditation See p. 6
	(No German Conversation Group meetings in February. Sorry for the inconvenience.)
Tuesday, Feb. 11	**10:00 AM Wild About Books—Storytime Fun!** See p. 3
	11:00 AM English Learners' Book Club See p. 8
	4:00 PM Tuesday Crafternoon See p. 3
	6:30 PM Book Buddies See p. 8
	7:00 PM The History & Impact of Financial Power: The Vampiric Rise, Fall & Rise Again of Fin. Capitalism See p. 7
	7:00 PM Board Game Night See p. 6 and 7
	7:00 PM Mt. Lebanon Writers Group Join other writers in sharing and editing work for personal use or for publication.
Wed., Feb. 12	**9:30, 10:15, 11:00 AM Book Babies** See p. 3
	10:00 AM International Women's Conversation Circles See p. 7
	12:30 PM Readers' Theater Rehearsal
	1:00 PM Threshold Choir Practice An ancient tradition of women singing a cappella at the bedside of those in need.
	1:30 PM Knitting Circle at the Library See p. 7
	3:30 PM Wii Wednesdays See p. 6
	6:00 PM EZ Math Workshop for 3rd-6th Graders See p. 3
	7:00 PM Independent Nights: a Library Film Series See p. 6
	7:00 PM Bienvenido—Have Fun While You Speak Spanish Practice your Spanish in an informal setting! Call the library to confirm.
	7:30 PM Yoga for You See p. 7
Thursday, Feb. 13	**9:30, 10:15, 11:00 AM Storytime for 2s & 3s** See p. 3
	10:00 AM Advanced Italian Conversation Join a lively and fun group reading and speaking the Italian language!
	1:00 PM Advances in Knee Replacement See p. 7
	7:00 PM Conversational Chinese and Chinese Culture Join us every Thursday to practice conversation and explore the culture.
	7:15 PM South Hills Flute Choir Flute players with at least three years of playing experience (all ages welcome) are invited to practice.
Friday, February 14	**10:00 AM Sensory Storytime** See p. 3
	3:15 PM Lebo Nerdfighters See p. 8
Saturday, Feb. 15	**10:00 AM Carnegie Screenwriters Group** This group engages in script readings, networking, and discussions of writing and filmmaking.
	1:00 PM South Hills Scrabble Club See p. 6
Sunday, Feb. 16	**1:30 PM Sunday Fundays** See p. 3
Monday, Feb. 17	**10:00 AM Morning Spanish Literature & Conversation Group** Speak and read in Spanish on a variety of topics.
	10:30 AM Shakespeare Readers See p. 8
	12:30 PM Readers' Theater Rehearsal
	1:00 PM Mt. Lebanon Genealogy Society See p. 7
	1:15 PM Hola Ninos! See p. 3
	7:00 PM Evening Book Group See p. 8
	7:30 PM Sahaja Meditation See p. 6
Tuesday, Feb. 18	**10:00 AM Wild About Books—Storytime Fun!** See p. 3
	11:00 AM English Learners' Book Club See p. 8
	2:00 PM Readers' Theater General Meeting Regular monthly meeting—find out more about this dedicated group of volunteers!
	4:00 PM Tuesday Crafternoon See p. 3
	6:30 PM Pajama Storytime See p. 3
	7:00 PM Klezlectic Concert See p. 7
	7:00 PM Library Board of Trustees Meeting All meetings of the Library Board are open to the public.
	7:15 PM Mystery Readers Book Club See p. 8
Wed., Feb. 19	**9:30, 10:15, 11:00 AM Book Babies** See p. 3
	10:00 AM English Conversation Class Practice your English in an informal setting. Please register at pkelley@gplc.org.

From *Crash Course in Marketing for Libraries: Second Edition* by Susan W. Alman and Sara Gillespie Swanson. Santa Barbara, CA: Libraries Unlimited. Copyright © 2015.

3:30 PM **Wii Wednesdays**   See p. 6

6:00 PM **EZ Math Workshop for 3rd-6th Graders**   See p. 3

6:30 PM **Folksong Sharing**   An informal group of lovers of folk songs.

7:00 PM **Just For Guys Book Discussion Group**   See p. 8

7:30 PM **Yoga for You**   See p. 7

Thursday, Feb. 20   9:15 AM **American History Book Discussion Group**   See p. 8

9:30, 10:15, 11:00 AM **Storytime for 2s & 3s**   See p. 3

10:00 AM **Advanced Italian Conversation**   Join a lively and fun group reading and speaking the Italian language!

12:30 PM **Readers' Theater Rehearsal**

7:00 PM **Bicycling in Wild & Wonderful West Virginia**   See p. 8

7:00 PM **Conversational Chinese and Chinese Culture**   Join us to practice conversational Chinese and explore Chinese culture. 7:15 PM South Hills Flute Choir Flute players with at least three years of playing experience (all ages welcome) are invited to practice.

Friday, February 21 12:30 PM **Readers' Theater Rehearsal**

5:00 PM **Teen Volunteer Night**   See p. 6

Saturday, Feb. 22   10:00 AM **Vegetable Gardening and Seed Sharing Event**   See p. 1

1:00 PM **South Hills Scrabble Club**   See p. 6

1:30 PM **The History & Impact of Financial Power: The Vampiric Rise, Fall & Rise Again of Fin. Capitalism**   See p. 7

Sunday, Feb. 23   1:30 PM **Sunday Fundays**   See p. 3

Monday, Feb. 24   10:00 AM **Morning Spanish Literature & Conversation Group**   Speak and read in Spanish on a variety of topics.

10:30 AM **Bonjour Les Amis**   See p. 3

10:30 AM **Shakespeare Readers**   See p. 8

12:30 PM **Readers' Theater Rehearsal**

1:15 PM **Hola Ninos!**   See p. 3

6:00 PM **Landscape Design Course**   See p. 1

7:00 PM **KidsLit Book Discussion Group**   See p. 8

7:30 PM **Sahaja Meditation**   See p. 6

Tuesday, Feb. 25   10:00 AM **Wild About Books—Storytime Fun!**   See p. 3

11:00 AM **English Learners' Book Club**   See p. 8

12:30 PM **Readers' Theater Rehearsal**

4:00 PM **Tuesday Crafternoon**   See p. 3

6:30 PM **Greater Pittsburgh Literacy Council Tutor Talk**   See p. 8

7:00 PM **Girls' Night Out**   See p. 8

7:00 PM **Board Game Night**   See p. 6 and 7

Wed., Feb. 26   9:30, 10:15, 11:00 AM **Book Babies**   See p. 3

10:00 AM **English Conversation Class**   Practice your English in an informal setting. Please register at pkelley@gplc.org.

3:30 PM **Wii Wednesdays**   See p. 6

4:00 PM **Lego Club**   See p. 3

6:00 PM **EZ Math Workshop for 3rd-6th Graders**   See p. 3

7:00 PM **Science Fiction Book Discussion Group**   See p. 8

7:00 PM **The American Civil War Era—Western Theater: A Geographic Focus**   See p. 8

7:00 PM **Bienvenido—Have Fun While You Speak Spanish**   Practice your Spanish in an informal setting! Call the library to confirm mtg.

7:30 PM **Yoga for You**   See p. 7

Thursday, Feb. 27   9:30, 10:15, 11:00 AM **Storytime for 2s & 3s**   See p. 3

10:00 AM **Advanced Italian Conversation**   Join a lively and fun group reading and speaking the Italian language!

7:00 PM **Conversational Chinese and Chinese Culture**   Join us to practice conversational Chinese and explore Chinese culture. All levels.

7:15 PM **South Hills Flute Choir**   Flute players with at least three years of playing experience (all ages welcome) are invited to practice.

7:30 PM **French Conversation**   Practice your French in an informal setting. New members always welcome to this language group!

Friday, February 28 10:00 AM **Book Chat**   See p. 8

SOUTH HILLS SCRABBLE CLUB
Saturdays, February 1, 8, 15, and 22
1:00pm

This club welcomes adults and kids ages 10 and up for an afternoon of friendly competition, in cooperation with Mt. Lebanon Public Library.

WII WEDNESDAYS
Wednesday, February 5, 12, 19, and 26
3:30pm

 Come play Nintendo classics and new Wii U games while enjoying snacks! (Kids ages 10 and up, no registration required.)

OTAKU LEBO
Thursday, February 6, 3:15pm

The Otaku Lebo Asian pop culture club for middle and high school students meets on the first Thursday of every month when school is in session.

BOARD GAME NIGHT
Tuesdays, February 11 and 25, 7:00pm

Settlers of Catan, Dominion, Carcassonne? New to the library, it's a fun night of strategy and competition playing Euro-style board games. This group is intended for high school students through adults. If you're a seasoned gamer, feel free to bring your own games; if you're new to this style of play, here are some examples of what will be available:

• Worker placement games (Settlers of Catan, Agricola)
• Deck builders (Dominion, Ascension)
• Cooperative games (Arkham Horror, Flash Point)

Join us to challenge yourself in friendly competition and meet some new Meeple.

TEEN VOLUNTEER NIGHT
Friday, February 21, 5:00pm

Students interested in receiving five hours of volunteer service (great opportunity for National Honor Society candidates) can sign up for this after-hours opportunity. Pizza and snacks will be available. Sign up at the Adult Reference Desk and pick up a registration packet (liability waiver and medical release). All forms must be turned in to the library before students can participate in the event (limited to 30).

GOOD FRIENDS: FOOD FOR THE SOUL
Monday, February 3, 7:00pm

We all know our friends make us feel good, but did you know they are also good for us? Chris Mabon presents a workshop and will discuss the five essential friendships we need to enrich our lives.

For Ms. Mabon, 22 years of marriage and raising two kids left her little time to connect with girlfriends in a meaningful way. When her husband died suddenly, she took inventory of herself, her relationships and her place in the world. She was embraced and comforted by friends, neighbors and members of the community who helped her to heal and move forward. She is currently working on a manuscript, *Comfort Food – One Woman's Journey to Understand the Meaning and Significance of Friendship.*

SAHAJA MEDITATION
Mondays, February 3, 10, 17, and 24
7:30pm

Discover the beauty within with simple meditation techniques. Meditation improves physical, emotional, psychological, social, and spiritual health and brings out a well-rounded personality, if practiced regularly. These classes are offered free of charge or obligation and no reservations are required.

MYTHS AND FACTS ABOUT HOSPICE CARE
Tuesday, February 4, 7:00pm

Join Barbara Ivanko, president and CEO of Family Hospice & Palliative Care, for a frank discussion of hospice care: what it is, where it happens, how it is accessed, how it is being impacted by the Affordable Care Act, and how it can benefit you and your loved ones. The program will close with a presentation by Pittsburgh Threshold Choir, which honors an ancient tradition of women singing a cappella at the bedside. They practice at Mt. Lebanon Public Library.

CREATIVE CONNECTIONS: Origami
Wednesday, February 5, 2:00pm

Join us on the first Wednesday of the month for programs especially suited for adults ages 50 and over. All *Creative Connections* programs are free and open to the public. Come early and socialize! This month's program: Origami.

INDEPENDENT NIGHTS: A LIBRARY FILM SERIES
Wednesdays, February 5 and 12, 7:00pm

See Richard Linklater's Before Sunrise/Sunset/Midnight Trilogy on three evenings. Your host for the series is local film historian Elaine Wertheim.

Richard Linklater made "Before Sunrise" with Ethan Hawke and Julie Delpy in 1995. Since Linklater, Hawke, and Delpy enjoyed their very collaborative filmmaking experience, they reunited to co-write "Before Sunset" in 2004, which picked up the story nine years after Jesse and Celine had promised each other to meet up again six months after their meeting in

Vienna. Another nine years later, Linklater "got the band back together," they packed bags for Greece, and made "Before Midnight." Join us for all three parts of this highly original trilogy set in stunning European locations.

YOGA FOR YOU
Wednesdays, February 5, 12, 19, and 26, 7:30pm

Yoga is a practice that benefits all ages and body types. Join us for a basic 60-minute flow class for all levels. Both beginners and experienced practitioners will benefit physically and mentally from the training. We will begin with a warm-up of Sun A and B, then move to standing poses before ending with a floor series. The classes will be led by certified teachers at South Hills Power Yoga. Each participant should have a yoga mat, a small hand towel, and water, if desired. Feel free to bring any questions you have about yoga to the class as well. It is free and no pre-registration is necessary.

LEAGUE OF WOMEN VOTERS
LUNCHTIME SERIES
Thursday, February 6, 12:30pm

At this regular monthly meeting the group will be reviewing proposed studies. Members should check the weekly email blast for further updates. All are welcome to attend, whether or not a member. Anyone with questions should contact Maureen Mamula at 412-760-9642.

THE HISTORY & IMPACT OF FINANCIAL POWER: THE VAMPIRIC RISE, FALL & RISE AGAIN OF FINANCIAL CAPITALISM
Tuesday, February 11, 7:00pm; Saturday, February 22, 1:30pm

This ongoing series is an in-depth examination and evaluation in an attempt to draw conclusions from the historical, political, and economic roots of the Great Depression and the Great Financial Crisis of 2008. We will be examining the period between 1964 and 2014 to bring our historical context up to date and to provide some in-depth understanding of the economic, social, political and military issues confronting our world in the coming decades.

As we discuss the issues to be faced in the coming decades, we will proceed as though we are a non-partisan think-tank attempting to develop and provide policy advice to national leaders. This should be an entertaining exercise where all participants will be afforded the opportunity to provide leadership and guidance.

BOARD GAME NIGHT
Tuesdays, February 11 and 25, 7:00pm

Settlers of Catan, Dominion, Carcassonne? New to the library, it's a fun night of strategy and competition playing Euro-style board games. This group is intended for high

school students through adults. If you're a seasoned gamer, feel free to bring your own games; if you're new to this style of play, here are some examples of what will be available:

• Worker placement games (Settlers of Catan, Agricola)
• Deck builders (Dominion, Ascension)
• Cooperative games (Arkham Horror, Flash Point)

Join us to challenge yourself in friendly competition and meet some new Meeple.

INTERNATIONAL WOMEN'S CONVERSATION CIRCLES
Wednesday, February 12, 10:00am

If you recently moved to Mt. Lebanon from another country, please join us for tea, refreshments, and conversation at Mt. Lebanon Public Library. Learn about your community while you make new friends! New women residents are welcome to practice their English while they learn about local activities and services available for themselves and their children. All women are welcome to meet their new neighbors from around the world, share information about our community, and learn more about the diverse cultures that enrich Mt. Lebanon. The program is presented in cooperation with the Greater Pittsburgh Literacy Council.

KNITTING CIRCLE AT THE LIBRARY
Wednesday, February 12, 1:30pm

Do you or your child enjoy knitting? Crocheting? Handwork? If so, come and enjoy working together — parents and homeschooled children as well as other adults are welcome. Learn new skills, share your expertise, and make friends during this daytime group!

ADVANCES IN KNEE REPLACEMENT
Thursday, February 13, 1:00pm

Thomas F. Brockmeyer, M.D., Ph.D., orthopedic surgeon, will discuss advances in knee replacement healing. Dr. Brockmeyer belongs to The Orthopedic Group of Mt. Lebanon, Charleroi, Jefferson and Uniontown. Light refreshments will be served.

MT. LEBANON GENEALOGY SOCIETY
Monday, February 17, 1:00pm

Join others in discussing family history and pick up tips on research. New members welcome!

KLEZLECTIC CONCERT
Tuesday, February 18, 7:00pm

The quartet Klezlectic specializes in klezmer music, but also mixes in American, Latin and Balkan music for a very lively brew of truly sweet genres. This Pittsburgh-based group dazzles and swings their way through every performance for fans of all ages.

8

BICYCLING IN WILD & WONDERFUL WEST VIRGINIA
Thursday, February 20, 7:00pm

Join Mt. Lebanon residents Doug Ettiger, Bill Kutzer and Dan Mottsman as they share and show last July's week-long cycling adventure on various Rails to Trails routes in West Virginia. This trio of casual bicyclists will describe their eight-day adventure highlighted by the Greenbrier River, Blackwater Canyon and Decker's Creek Trails, sharing their unique experiences with trip photos. This was not a point-to-point trip, but rather one that required automobile logistics and lodging location coordination.

With the Morgantown area only a one-hour drive away, you could plan your own one- to eight-day adventure. Doug, Bill and Dan will offer tips on pre-planning, resources, lodging options, support groups, directions, and local day trips to get you in shape. A Q&A session will follow.

GREATER PITTSBURGH LITERACY COUNCIL TUTOR TALK
Tuesday, February 25, 6:30pm

GPLC tutors are invited to a monthly "Tutor Talk" with Peggi Kelley, South Hills area coordinator. It is presented by the Greater Pittsburgh Literacy Council in cooperation with Mt. Lebanon Public Library.

THE AMERICAN CIVIL WAR ERA - WESTERN THEATER: A GEOGRAPHIC FOCUS
Wednesday, February 26, 7:00pm

This lecture/discussion series focuses on events prior to and during the American Civil War in the much neglected Western Theater, which includes the Midwest and Trans-Mississippi. Emphasis will be placed on Union and Confederate Theater strategy, Theater political and military leadership and the geo-political factors that help understand this very large area of conflict. Battlefield tactics are not a focus — the two books listed below with their maps adequately cover battlefield details. You may join the presentation series at any time since the sessions are "topic oriented"; attending previous sessions is not a requirement.

Presenter Rodger Duffy has a master's degree in political geography from Northwestern University and taught the subject at DePaul University in Chicago and the University of Wisconsin-Whitewater.

Power Point presentations will be used to enrich the sessions. Suggested readings include *Grant Moves South* by Bruce Catton and *Battle Cry of Freedom* by James McPherson.

Book Discussions

mtlebanonlibrary.org/readers/bookgroups

Shakespeare Readers
Mondays, February 3, 17, and 24, 10:30am
Please ask at the reference desk for the selection.

English Learners' Book Club
Tuesdays, February 4, 11, 18, and 25, 11:00am
The books and short stories will be available to participants through the library. Please register with Peggi Kelley at 412-531-3004 or pkelley@gplc.org, Greater Pittsburgh Literacy Council.

Crazy for Comics! (second and third grade)
Wednesday, February 5, 6:30pm
Please ask for the selection in the children's library.

American History Book Discussion Group
Thursdays, February 6 and 20, 9:15am
The selection is *From Colony to Superpower,* Chapters 14 & 15 (Feb. 6); Chapters 16 &17 (Feb. 20).

Morning Book Discussion Group
Monday, February 10, 10:30am
The selection is *Uncle Tom's Cabin* by Harriet B. Stowe.

American Girl Book Club (grades 2, 3 & 4)
Monday, February 10, 6:30pm
Please ask for the selection in the children's library.

Book Buddies (kindergarten & first grade)
Tuesday, February 11, 6:30pm
Please ask for the selection in the children's library.

Lebo Nerdfighters (college and high school)
Friday, February 14, 3:15pm
MORE than just a book group, an open discussion of mature teen literature and enjoyment of ALL things nerdy.

Evening Book Group
Monday, February 17, 7:00pm
This month's selection is *The Dinner* by Herman Koch.

Mystery Readers Book Club
Tuesday, February 18, 7:15pm
Please ask at the reference desk for the selection.

Just For Guys Book Discussion Group (boys ages 10 - 13 and their dads [or other caring male adults])
Wednesday, February 19, 7:00pm
The selection is *The Fourth Stall* by Chris Rylander.

KidsLit Book Discussion Group (adults)
Monday, February 24, 7:00pm
Please ask at the children's desk for the selection.

Girls' Night Out (girls ages 10 - 13 and their moms [or other caring female adults])
Tuesday, February 25, 7:00pm
Please ask for the selection in the children's library.

Science Fiction Book Discussion Group
Wednesday, February 26, 7:00pm
The selections are novel *A Scanner Darkly* by Philip K. Dick and short fiction *Memory Dog* by Kathleen Ann Goonan and *Bring the Jubilee* by Ward Moore.

Book Chat (seniors [formerly PALS Book Group])
Friday, February 28, 10:00am
Mingle with good books and neighbors each month. Expand yourself with thought-provoking discussions of books from different genres. The selection is *Miss Peregrine's Home for Peculiar Children* by Ransom Riggs.

Published by Friends of the Mt. Lebanon Library

Library Director: Cynthia K. Richey
Friends President: William F. Lewis
Newsletter Editor: Kelly Sterling Lotter

Mt. Lebanon Public Library Assn
16 Castle Shannon Boulevard
Pittsburgh, PA 15228-2252
Phone: 412-531-1912
Fax: 412-531-1161
www.mtlebanonlibrary.org

Library Hours:
Monday-Thursday 9-9
Friday-Saturday 9-5
Sunday 1-5

Non-Profit Org.
U.S. Postage
PAID
Pittsburgh, PA
Permit No. 2358

Current Resident or

Thanks to the **Allegheny Regional Asset District** for its support. RAD reinforces our ability to sustain a high level of programming and services by providing more than 24% of the library's operating funds.

The Friends of the Mt. Lebanon Library is a nonprofit organization, organized under IRS Code, Section 501(c)(3), managed solely by volunteers, that offers added financial support and assistance to the library.

The official registration and financial information on Friends of the Mt. Lebanon Library may be obtained from the Pennsylvania Department of State by calling toll free, within Pennsylvania, 1 (800) 732-0999. Registration does not imply endorsement.

Look for your membership renewal reminder postcard in the mail. We hope you will continue your support of the library as a Friends member.

Membership is a minimum of $15 per person and can be mailed or dropped off at the library circulation desk. Make checks payable to "Friends of the Mt. Lebanon Library."

A GREAT GIFT IDEA Sign up a friend, family member, or neighbor as a FRIEND. It's a great, inexpensive gift for anyone who loves to read or loves the library. Friends receive an entire year (10 issues) of the newsletter—a great way to support the library and keep up to date on library events.

Yes! I want to renew/join as a Friend of the Mt. Lebanon Public Library.
I am ____ renewing ____ becoming a new member
____ giving a membership to someone as a gift (please use the recipient's information for the form below)

Enclosed is my tax-deductible check payable to *Friends of the Mt. Lebanon Library* in the amount of:
____ $100 ____ $50 ____ $25 ____ $15 ____ Other _____

Name: _____
Address: _____
City: _____ State: _____ Zip: _____
E-mail: _____ Phone: _____
Your name (if this membership is a gift) _____

Please indicate how you would prefer to receive your Friends newsletter:
☐ **in the mail only**   ☐ **by e-mail only**   ☐ **both mail and e-mail**

Please mail or drop off your form and check at the library: 16 Castle Shannon Blvd., Pittsburgh, PA 15228-2252.   **NL**

Appendix J

Sample Friends of the Library Newsletters

MT. LEBANON PUBLIC LIBRARY : **more friends**

Friends of the Mt. Lebanon Library Newsletter

December 2012 ● Volume XXXIX ● Issue 4

Renew That Chair!

Wooden Chair CHAIRity Project at Mt. Lebanon Public Library

Decorated chairs will be available to buy April 19, 2013

In October 2012, the library received new seating, made possible through generous donations specifically for that purpose. The old and worn-beyond-repair upholstered seating from 1997 was donated to charity. More than 125 wooden chairs remain in the library at present, but there are big plans to give them a new life and to raise funds for the library at the same time.

Creative members of the public are invited to take a chair (or two) home to refurbish/decorate and return to the library in April as part of Mt. Lebanon Public Library's CHAIRity event.

Chairs can be taken from the library for refurbishment immediately after logging them out at the Circulation Desk. They may be decorated in any way (painted, stenciled, covered in decoupage, etc.) with any theme.*

Renewed chairs need to be returned to the library a few days before the special after-hours CHAIRity event on Friday, April 19, 2013, at which time the chairs will be offered for sale. (Artists will set their own prices on the chairs they've decorated.)

All proceeds from the sale of the renewed chairs benefit Mt. Lebanon Public Library.

*The sky's the limit! Decorating ideas include (but are not limited to): book/reading themes, Pittsburgh sports teams, school colors and logos, princesses/pirates, flora and fauna, suits of cards, quotes, etc...

Brews for a Chili Night III - January 26
Tickets on sale starting December 1!

Attention beer aficionados, chili lovers, and fans of the library: Don't miss the fun at the next Brews for a Chili Night event!

Taste fine brews and delicious varieties of homemade chili at the library and enjoy the live music of Cello Fury on this festive evening. Cost is $30 per person and attendance is limited.

Make your holiday gift-giving easy and pick up your tickets in advance! Ticket price includes an evening of complimentary beers, hearty chili, and savory snacks. The chili chefs will rustle up big batches of their best chili and you can bet both vegetarians and carnivores will be delighted with the results.

 ROTARY POINSETTIA SALE — Support the Dormont-Mt. Lebanon-Castle Shannon Rotary Club's 4th Annual Poinsettia Sale, benefiting the library. For just $10 each, you will receive a fabulous 6-1/2 inch foil-wrapped pot of red, pink, or white poinsettias. The sale runs **through Sunday, Dec. 16** at the library.

Inside this issue

For article ideas, etc., please send email to kelly.lotter@gmail.com.

Keep up with events at the library via mtlebanonlibrary.org, Facebook, and Twitter!

To register for any programs or for more information, call the library at 412-531-1912 or email events@ mtlebanonlibrary.org.

The Book Cellar
Bookstore
Lower level of the library

Monday 10-8
Tuesday 10-8
Wednesday 10-8
Thursday 10-8
Friday & Saturday 10-4
Sunday closed

HAPPY 4TH BIRTHDAY BOOK CELLAR!
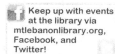

Wooden Chair CHAlRity Project at Mt. Lebanon Public Library

RENEW THAT CHAIR!

Decorated Chairs for Sale on April 19, 2013

In October 2012 the library received new seating, made possible through generous donations for that purpose. The old and worn-beyond-repair upholstered seating from 1997 was donated to charity. Over 125 wooden chairs remain in the library at present, but we have big plans to give them a new life and to raise funds for the library at the same time.

1. Creative members of the public are invited to take a chair (or two) home to refurbish and return to the library in April as part of Mt. Lebanon Public Library's CHAlRity event.

    a. Chairs can be taken from the library refurbishment immediately after logging them out at the Circulation Desk.

    b. Chairs may be decorated in any way with any theme* (painted, stenciled, covered in decoupage, etc).

2. Renewed chairs need to be returned to the library a few days before the CHAlRity event on Friday, April 19.

    a. Artists set their own prices on the chairs they've decorated. Chairs are offered for sale starting Friday, 4/19/2013 at a special after-hours event.

    b. All proceeds from the sale of the RENEWED CHAIRS benefit Mt. Lebanon Public Library.

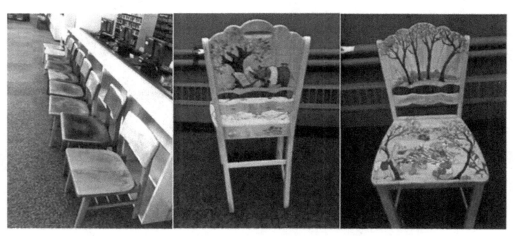

I Overdue chairs waiting to be renewed.   Two views of a renewed chair.

*The sky's the limit! Decorating ideas include (but are not limited to): booklreading themes, Pittsburgh sports teams, school colors and logos, princesses/pirates, flora and fauna, suits of cards, quotes . . .

Before   After

Come to Mt. Lebanon Public Library's
CHAIRity Sale and Social !

Over 70 chairs have been renewed by professional artists
& creative members of the public.

Friday, April 19, 6 p.m.

Before   After

Come to Mt. Lebanon Public Library's
CHAIRity Sale and Social !

Over 70 chairs have been renewed by professional artists
& creative members of the public.

Friday, April 19, 6 p.m.

CHAIR LOG

Wooden Chair CHAIRity Project at Mt. Lebanon Public Library
RENEW THAT CHAIR!
Decorated Chairs for Sale on April 19, 2013

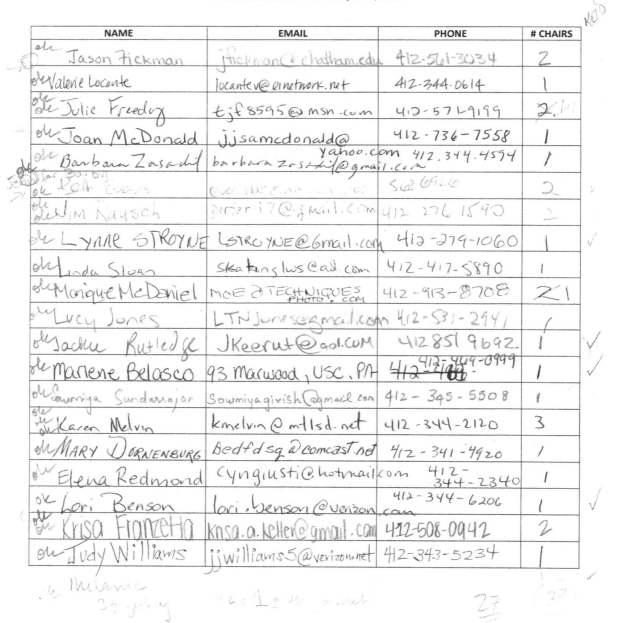

NAME	EMAIL	PHONE	# CHAIRS
Jason Fickman	jfickman@chatham.edu	412-561-3034	2
Valerie Locante	locantev@einetwork.net	412-344-0614	1
Julie Freedey	tjf8595@msn.com	412-571-9199	2
Joan McDonald	jjsamcdonald@yahoo.com	412-736-7558	1
Barbara Zasadil	barbarazosadil@gmail.com	412.344.4594	1
Beth Evans	eva.the.e...	56.6926	2
Jim Raysch	porter17@gmail.com	412 276 1590	2
Lynne Stroyne	Lstroyne@gmail.com	412-279-1060	1
Linda Sloan	skatinglws@ad.com	412-417-5890	1
Monique McDaniel	moe@techniques photo.com	412-913-8708	2 1
Lucy Jones	LTNJones@gmail.com	412-531-2941	1
Jackie Rutledge	JKeerut@aol.com	412 851 9692	1
Marlene Belasco	93 Marwood, USC, PA	412-469-0999	1
Sowmiya Sundarrajan	Sowmiyagirish@gmail.com	412-345-5508	1
Karen Melvin	kmelvin@mtlsd.net	412-344-2120	3
MARY DORNENBURG	Bedfdsq@comcast.net	412-341-4920	1
Elena Redmond	cyngiusti@hotmail.com	412-344-2340	1
Lori Benson	lori.benson@verizon.com	412-344-6206	1
Krisa Franzetta	krisa.a.keller@gmail.com	412-508-0942	2
Judy Williams	jjwilliams5@verizon.net	412-343-5234	1

27

From *Crash Course in Marketing for Libraries: Second Edition* by Susan W. Alman and Sara Gillespie Swanson. Santa Barbara, CA: Libraries Unlimited. Copyright © 2015.

 Our CHAIRity Sale and Social takes place from 6:00 – 7:30 p.m. this Friday, April 19. Please join us for this fun library celebration!

Have other plans that evening, but see a chair you love? Ask at the Circulation Desk about placing an early-bird bid. Others may outbid you at the silent auction, but give it a try!

100% of the proceeds from the CHAIRity benefit Mt. Lebanon Public Library. Thank you for your support!!

From *Crash Course in Marketing for Libraries: Second Edition* by Susan W. Alman and Sara Gillespie Swanson. Santa Barbara, CA: Libraries Unlimited. Copyright © 2015.

Mt Lebanon Public Library
celebrates
National Library Week

CHAIRity Sale and Social

6:00 p.m. — 7:30 p.m.
April 19, 2013

Bid on the amazing chairs, enjoy live music, and mingle with your neighbors!

MT. LEBANON
PUBLIC
LIBRARY :more

Mark your calendar for these red-letter dates at Mt. Lebanon Public Library!

- Mt. Leb. HS AP-US History Series, April 24-May 29
- Astronomy & Stargazing for Families, Thursday, May 16
- Summer Reading Clubs for all! Start Monday, June 10
- Garden Party, Saturday, July 6*
- Garden Tour, Sunday, Sunday, July 7*
- Concerts in the Courtyards series on Thursdays:
  Aug 1—Olga Watkins Band - Original Blues, Soul & Funk
  Aug 8—Hardbark Sycamore - Folk, Rock & Acoustic
  Aug 15—Resonance Trio - Caribbean/Jazz Quintet
  Aug 22—Jeff Berman's Eye 2 Eye - Worldly Folk-Jazz Dulcimer & Percussion Duo
  Aug 29—Mt Lebanon High School String Quartet
- Beer Garden Bash, Saturday, Aug 24*
- A Novel Affair: The Great Gatsby, Saturday, October 12*
  Mt. Lebanon Public Library's Sensational Speakeasy

*These events are fundraisers to benefit the library.

Thank you for coming!

Mt. Lebanon Public Library
16 Castle Shannon Boulevard
Pittsburgh, PA 15228-2252
412-531-1912
www.mtlebanonlibrary.org

WELCOME TO CHAIRity!

The sale of approximately 70 creatively-renewed wooden library chairs takes place this evening!

From the artist-suggested starting price, a silent auction will run from 6:00 p.m. until 7:30 p.m. Bid early and bid often.... or *Buy It Now!*

Heartfelt thanks to the talented artists who donated their time and the materials to transform these chairs into works of art:

Jean Benson	Beth Evans	Terri Pollock
Marlene Belasco	Lynne Stroyne	Wendy Spigle
Jacqueline Rutledge	Melanie Szigethy	Betty Disque
Hannah Jones	Adrienne Hagins	Julie Hagins
Joni McDonald	Mary Dornenburg	Scheiferstein
Frances Marze	Sue Kimutis	Erin Rutter
Barbara Zasadil	Alicia Scheiferstein	Julie Freedy
Margot Stein	Emily Adair	Veronica Guns
Amy Quinlan	Rosemarie Mazza	Anna Conway
Monique McDaniel	Hanna Edvardsson	Patty Siegfried
Michelle Ivan	Gretchen Donnelly	Somiya
Shannon Berkheiser	Ian Stevenson	Krisa Franzetta
Barbara Keller	Ali Rovers	Kathryn White
Maureen White	Maria Mangano	Greg Rose
Karen Gottschall	Linda Sebastian	Judy Sombar
Girl Scout Troop 50609	Stephen Douglas	Erin Long
Erin Leach & Family	Linda Sebastian	Ellie Wilcox
Barb Alsko & Ella Winters	Sam Ditch	
Valerie Locante & Mike Lillis	Ilene Iskoe & Linda Sloan	
Jessica Turner & Nina Barbetti	GS Troops 51157 & 50751	
Elena Redmond & Virginia Giusti	Kathy, Caroline & Nam Vo	
Remade Renegade aka Amy Miller		
Claudia Jester & Clarissa Angelopoulos		
Jaclyn Wood, Alicia Koloski, Lucy Jones,		
Jenna Keeling & Jay Kuntz		

A standing ovation for the talented musicians:

Act 1: Jefferson Middle School Jazz Band
Ariana Mandros, Kelly Hois, Alex Baran, Harrison Greenbaum, Aaron Corcos, Branwen Pollett, Scott McDanel, Maxwell Ernest, Eoin Wilson-Manion, Allen Fry, Catie Rogan, Joe Dameron, Alex Vandale, Ajay Wadhwani, Jeremy Farbman, Alex Dornback, Dylan Marfisi, Nico Ricciutti, Bryce Brandenstein, Robbie Doncourt, Alexis Schulte-Albert under the direction of Mr. Doug Reichenfeld

Act 2: Mt. Lebanon High School String Quartet
Philip Clippinger, Sophie Yang, Jacob Hitt, Tess Clippinger under the direction of Mr. Robert Vogel

Act 3: South Hills Flute Choir

Sweet kudos for the bakers:

Caroline Ingalls	Jill Martin
Katie McGinley	Sharon Verminski
Linda Vietmeier	

And thanks to:

Learning Express Toys of Mt. Lebanon in the Galleria for their generous auction donation.

Important Notes:

- The silent auction begins at 6:00 p.m. Bidding will end in three phases: Group 1 ends at 7:00 p.m., Group 2 ends at 7:15 p.m., and Group 3 ends at 7:30 p.m.

- After the auction has ended, check the chair to see who won. Once you have paid for your chair at the Circulation Desk, you may take your chair home.

- You may claim the purchase price of the chair (less $40 for the value of the wooden chair) as a charitable deduction.

- All proceeds benefit Mt. Lebanon Public Library. Thank you for your support!

Pod Volunteer completes buyer initial, name & amount

Cashier completes how paid w/ amount & tender & signs "by"

(S)

Smith, Robert

Jennifer

You may claim the purchase price of the chair (less $40 for the value of the wooden chair) as a charitable deduction.

NO. 54840①

DOLLARS $ 40

☐ FOR RENT
☐ FOR ___ Rose in Bloom

ACCOUNT		HOW PAID	
AMT OF ACCOUNT		CASH	
AMT PAID		CHECK	40 00
BALANCE DUE		CC	

BY Mary

Pod Volunteer completes buyer initial, name & amount

Cashier completes how paid w/ amount & tender & signs "by"

(S)

Smith, Robert

You may claim the purchase price of the chair (less $40 for the value of the wooden chair) as a charitable deduction.

NO. 54840②

DOLLARS $ 50

☐ FOR RENT
☐ FOR Go Dog, Go!

ACCOUNT		HOW PAID	
AMT OF ACCOUNT		CASH	
AMT PAID		CHECK	50 00
BALANCE DUE		CC	

BY Mary

Pod Volunteer completes buyer initial, name & amount

Cashier completes how paid w/ amount & tender & signs "by"

(S)

Smith, Robert

You may claim the purchase price of the chair (less $40 for the value of the wooden chair) as a charitable deduction.

NO. 54840③

DOLLARS $ 75

☐ FOR RENT
☐ FOR ___ Sit & Knit Awhile

ACCOUNT		HOW PAID	
AMT OF ACCOUNT		CASH	
AMT PAID		CHECK	75 00
BALANCE DUE		CC	

BY Mary

Pod Volunteer completes buyer initial, name & amount

Cashier completes how paid w/ amount & tender & signs "by"

(S)

Smith, Robert

You may claim the purchase price of the chair (less $40 for the value of the wooden chair) as a charitable deduction.

NO. 54840④

DOLLARS $ 100

☐ FOR RENT
☐ FOR On the Reef

ACCOUNT		HOW PAID	
AMT OF ACCOUNT		CASH	
AMT PAID		CHECK	100 00
BALANCE DUE		CC	

BY Mary

From *Crash Course in Marketing for Libraries: Second Edition* by Susan W. Alman and Sara Gillespie Swanson. Santa Barbara, CA: Libraries Unlimited. Copyright © 2015.

Procedure for Silent Auction

Chairs are arranged in groups, or pods, of 10. A volunteer is assigned to each pod. The volunteer will be an active host, engaging guests, answering questions and encouraging them to bid.

The silent auction will last an hour. The opening bid was set by the artist; the Buy It Now price set by our director, Cynthia Richey in consultation with experts. Bid should be made in $10 increments. A Buy It Now bid can be made any time-and that ends the auction for that chair. (The buyer could then pay for the chair early, if desired.)

At 10 and 5 minutes before the auction ends, announcements will be made to the guests. Once the announcement is made that the auction is closed, the pod volunteer will collect the bid sheets and identify the winners.

The pod volunteer will:

1. Circle the winning bid on the bid sheets, keeping them on the clipboard
2. Write the winners' names on the yellow hold slips, placing them on the chair seats
3. Complete the payment receipts in triplicate with the winner's last initial, name, and winning bid
4. Run these slips to the Circ Desk for payment by the winners, where the slips will be divided by last initial
5. Return to the pod to release chairs to the winners after checking that the chairs have been paid for and taking the yellow slip
6. Save yellow slips on clipboard.

Winners will:

1. See their names on the yellow hold slips on the chairs
2. Go to Circ Desk to the line with their last initial (A-J, K-P, Q-Z) to pay
3. Pay with cash or check at that line, otherwise go to cash register with triplicated receipt to pay by credit card
4. Receive the top and yellow copies of the receipt

5. Give yellow receipt to pod volunteer in exchange for chair

6. Take chair and retain blue receipt.

Cashiers will:

1. Sort triplicate receipts by last name initial

2. Collect cash or check payment, using a cash box.

3. Mark "how paid," sign name, and keep pink copy OR send winner to cash register to pay by credit card, giving winner ALL three copies of receipt to give to CC cashier. CC cashier will then process payment, mark "how paid," sign name, and keep pink copy.

FAQ:

1. How do I pay? You may pay by cash, check or Mastercard/Visa. No debit cards, AmEx, or Discover can be accepted.

2. Can I get a charitable deduction? You may claim the purchase price of the chair (less $40 for the value of the wooden chair) as a charitable deduction.

3. Can I pick up my chair later? Yes, but please pay for it tonight and we will mark it as paid-to be picked up later.

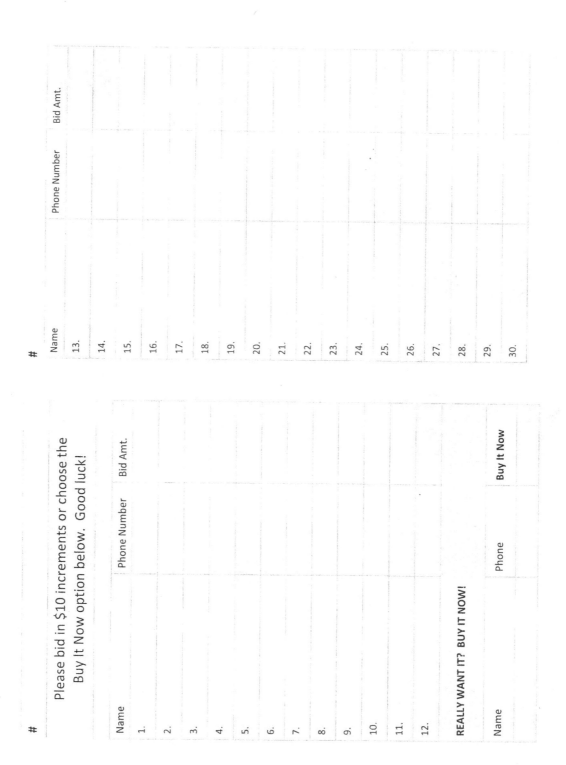

A PUBLICATION OF THE FRIENDS OF McMINNVILLE PUBLIC LIBRARY

Among Friends

March 2014—May 2014   Spring 2014

2014

FRIENDS OF
McMINNVILLE
PUBLIC LIBRARY

Author Ismet Prcic will discuss his book, *Shards*, on Thursday, May 1, at 7:30 p.m. in the Austin Reading Room at Nicholson Library at Linfield College.

The reading is a part of this year's MacReads program and PLACE (Program for Liberal Arts and Civic Engagement) initiative.

In its 10th year, MacReads is a community-wide book reading and discussion that culminates in a presentation by the author. Schools, book clubs and residents throughout Yamhill County are encouraged to participate. Books will be available for purchase and signing at the event, which is open to the public.

"Shards" describes the story of a young Bosnian, also named Ismet Prcic, who has recently fled the city of Tuzla during the Bosnian war. He escapes Tuzla with a theatre troupe on its way to Scotland and ultimately finds his way into the U.S. Throughout the story, Ismet, also known as Izzy, battles the guilt he feels for leaving his family behind. To deal with this guilt and make peace with his past, Izzy writes down all of his memories, thoughts and feelings. One aspect of his writing includes a viewpoint of another young man, real or imagined, named Mustafa, who stayed in Bosnia to fight. The result of these conflicting viewpoints and experiences reveals a truthful description of one man's journey to make sense of the life he left behind in Bosnia, while at the same time piecing his life together in the U.S.

Prcic was born in Tuzla, Bosnia-Herzegovina, in 1977 and lived there until he immigrated to the U.S. in 1996. He received a Master of Fine Arts from the University of California, Irvine. He is also a recipient of the 2010 National Endowment for the Arts and fellow for the 2011 Sundance Screenwriting Lab. In addition, Prcic won the 2013 Oregon Book Awards' Ken Kesey Award for "Shards." Prcic lives in Portland with his wife.

MacReads uses a common book to create community conversations that cross lines of generation and acquaintance. It is sponsored by Nicholson Library, McMinnville Public Library, Third Street Books and the Linfield English Department.

This year's PLACE program, "Legacies of War," seeks to create a common space within the Linfield community to discuss the causes, consequences and legacies of war from a variety of perspectives and from an array of disciplines.

For more information, contact Susan Barnes Whyte, director of Linfield libraries, 503-883-2517.

Officers

Neil Kunze, President
Denise Patton, Vice President
Loretta Hawley, Treasurer
Berniece Owen, Secretary

Members at Large:
Carol Dodge
Judie Folgate
Samantha Jordan
Glenda Carter

Library

225 NW Adams St
McMinnville, OR 97128
www.maclibrary.org
libref@ci.mcminnville.or.us

Circulation:
503-435-5561
Reference:
503-435-5562
Children's:
503-435-5559

Monday: Closed
Tuesday: 10am - 8pm
Wednesday: 10am - 8pm
Thursday: 10am - 8pm
Friday: 10am - 5pm
Saturday: 1pm - 5pm
Sunday: 1pm - 5pm

Page 2

Book Donations: December 2013, January & February 2014

Celebration:

Susan Barnes-Whyte
When Women Were Birds, by Terry Tempest Williams
The More Beautiful World Our Hearts Know is Possible, by Charles Eisenstein
Works Cited: an alphabetical odyssey of mayhem and misbehavior, by Brandon R. Schrand
Ask Me: 100 essential poems, by William Stafford
The Osage Orange Tree, by William Stafford

Karlene & Jeff Peterson
The Green Vine, by Shannon Borg
Learning from Leonardo, by Fritjof Capra
Our America: A Hispanic History of the United States, by Felipe Fernandez-Armesto

Alexander Lee Shinoda
Baby Bear Sees Blue, by Ashley Wolff

Memorial:

Wendell Armstrong
The Tiny King, by Taro Miura
Night Light, by Nicholas Blechman
Abigail, by Catherine Rayner
Peck, Peck, Peck, by Lucy Cousins

Norma Jean Nelson
One Bowl Baking, by Yvonne Ruperti
Indian Cooking Unfolded, by Raghavan Iyer

Annie Six
Speak the Speech, Shakespeare's Monologues, by Rhona Silverbrush

---

Change in Leadership in the Board of Directors of the Friends of the McMinnville Public Library

Because of personal and business responsibilities, the President of our Board, Laurie Furch, resigned from the Board this past December. On behalf of the entire Board I would like to thank Laurie for her outstanding service to the Friends, including her serving this past year and a half as our President. Also, the Board is very appreciative of the wonderful program support provided by Laurie and her husband, Jason, through their business, Red Fox Bakery.

Since I had been serving as Vice President when Laurie resigned in December, I have moved into the role as President of the Board. Denise Patton, who had served as our Treasurer, was approved by the Board at our January meeting as the new Vice President.

In you are interested in learning more about the activities of the Friends of the McMinnville Public Library please send me an email at *kunze@sou.edu*. Also, you are always welcome to attend our Board meetings, which are held at 12 noon in the Carnegie Room of the Library on the second Thursday of every month (no meeting in August). Finally, do not forget to donate your quality used books for our bi-monthly book sales, which are held on the second Saturday of January, March, May, July, September and November. We also hope you will attend the members' preview sale which is held between 9-10 am before the sale is opened to the public at 10 am on Saturday.

Sincerely,
Neil Kunze, President of the Friends of McMinnville Public Library

---

Booklover's Tea Time

Please join the Library Foundation for the Booklover's Tea Time! The February snowstorm postponed the annual event, which will now occur on Saturday, April 19th. The Tea begins at 1pm at the Grand Ballroom on Third Street. Enjoy live music, an author reading by Heather Sharfeddin, a raffle, door prizes, tea sandwiches, scones, pastries, and tea.

Purchase tickets in advance at the McMinnville Public Library or at Oregon Stationers by April 15th. All proceeds from the event go to support the Library Foundation of McMinnville and its mission to support collections, information technology, and other capital needs of the McMinnville Public Library.

There are still tickets available, but the event nearly sold out last year... so get your tickets soon! Call the Library's Information Desk for more info: 503-435-5562

Friends of the Library Annual Potluck

You are invited to the Friends of the Library annual meeting potluck. Bring your "food" contribution to share. We hope to see you there!

What:	**Potluck & Friends of the Library meeting**
When:	**April 10, 2014 at 12:00 Noon**
Where:	**The home of Carol Dodge**
	914 NW Sunnywood Court
	McMinnville, Oregon

Poetry Night

Join the McMinnville Public Library and the Velvet Monkey Tea Room on Thursday, April 3rd for a night of William Stafford Poetry.

We will celebrate the William Stafford's centennial by reading his poetry and discussing his legacy.

The event is free and starts at 6 pm. For more information, contact Diane McMillen at diane.mcmillen@ci.mcminnville.or.us or call 503-435-5551.

Feel free to bring a poem to share, or simply join us for an excellent cup of tea. We hope to see you there!

March 2014

READ·LEARN·GROW·INQUIRE
McMINNVILLE·PUBLIC
L I B R A R Y
www.maclibrary.org
(503) 435 - 5562

Sunday 1pm-5pm	Monday Closed	Tuesday 10am-8pm	Wednesday 10am-8pm	Thursday 10am-8pm	Friday 10am-5pm	Saturday 1pm-5pm
		Teen Tech Week @ the Library March 9-15 is Teen Tech Week. It's a time for teens and parents to visit the library and learn more about the technology they can find there. Stop by the library to learn about downloading e-books, free access to online AP test prep, SAT prep, and much more!				*1* **First Saturday at the Library** 2:00pm Digging for Leprechaun's Gold
2 **Dramatic Writing and Reading Group** 5:00pm	*3* **Cat Coalition Meeting** 10:00am **Yamhill County Slow Food Meeting** 6:00pm	*4* **Emergent Reader Story Time (ages 4-6)** 10:00am **Writer's Support Group** 1:00pm	*5* **Toddler Story Time (ages 2-3)** 10:00am **Teen Council** 4:15pm **First Wednesday Book Club** 2:00pm	*6* **Babytime (ages 0-2)** 10:00am	*7* **Emergent Reader Story Time** 10:00am **Teen Gaming Night** 5:00pm	*8* **Book Sale** 10:00am-2:00pm Doors open at 9:00am for current Friends of the Library members
9 **Dramatic Writing and Reading Group** 5:00pm	*10* **La Leche Meeting** 9:00am **Mac ATC Make and Trade Group** 6:00pm	*11* **Emergent Reader Story Time** 10:00am **Autism Society of Oregon Workshop: Transitions** 4:00pm **Book Group** 7:00pm	*12* **Toddler Story Time (ages 2-3)** 10:00am **Watercolor Group** 12:30pm	*13* **Babytime (ages 0-2)** 10:00am **Friends Meeting** noon	*14* **Emergent Reader Story Time (ages 4-6)** 10:00am	*15*
16 **Dramatic Writing and Reading Group** 5:00pm	*17*	*18* **Writer's Support Group** 1:00pm	*19* **Kiddo's Play Time** 10:00am **Watercolor Group** 12:30pm	*20*	*21* **Children's Essay Contest** deadline 5:00pm	*22*
23 **Dramatic Writing and Reading Group** 5:00pm	*24* **Together Works LGBT support group** 6:00pm	*25* **Writer's Support Group** 1:00pm **Science Mania** 2:00pm (ages 9-12) **Neverland Book Club** 7:00pm	*26* **Kiddo's Play Time** 10:00am **Evergreen Science Program** 2:00pm **Watercolor Group** 12:30pm	*27* **Children's Art Party** 2:00pm **Native Plant Meeting** 7:00pm	*28* **No School Children's Movie** 2:00pm	*29*
30	*31*					

Story Time Break:
March 18-March 28
Special crafts in the Children's Room to celebrate Spring Break! (March 25-28)

2014 Children's Essay Contest

Sponsored by Friends of McMinnville Public Library

Essay Theme: What I liked about (title of book) and what I would change in it.

Contest Divisions: 1st - 2nd Graders
3rd - 4th Graders
5th - 6th Graders

Stop by the Library's Children's Room for more information
about the Children's Essay Contest.

April 2014

READ·LEARN·GROW·INQUIRE
McMINNVILLE·PUBLIC
LIBRARY
www.maclibrary.org   (503) 435 - 5562

Sunday 1pm-5pm	Monday Closed	Tuesday 10am-8pm	Wednesday 10am-8pm	Thursday 10am-8pm	Friday 10am-5pm	Saturday 1pm-5pm
		1 Emergent Reader Story Time (ages 4-6) 10:00am	**2** Toddler Story Time (ages 2-3) 10:00am First Wednesday Book Club 2:00pm	**3** Babytime (ages 0-2) 10:00am Poetry Night @ Velvet Monkey Tea 6:00pm	**4** Emergent Reader Story Time (ages 4-6) 10:00am Teen Gaming Night 5:00pm	**5**
6	**7** Yamhill County Slow Food Meeting 6:00pm	**8** Emergent Reader Story Time (ages 4-6) 10:00am Library Book Group 7:00pm	**9** Toddler Story Time (ages 2-3) 10:00am	**10** Babytime (ages 0-2) 10:00am Friends Meeting noon	**11** Emergent Reader Story Time (ages 4-6) 10:00am	**12**
13 national library week	**14** La Leche Meeting 9:00am Mac ATC Make and Trade Group 6:00pm	**15** Emergent Reader Story Time (ages 4-6) 10:00am	**16** Toddler Story Time (ages 2-3) 10:00am	**17** Babytime (ages 0-2) 10:00am	**18** Emergent Reader Story Time (ages 4-6) 10:00am	**19** Booklover's Tea Time @ the McMinnville Grand Ballroom 1:00pm
20	**21** Together Works LGBT support group 6:00pm	**22** Emergent Reader Story Time (ages 4-6) 10:00am	**23** Toddler Story Time (ages 2-3) 10:00am *World Book Night* www.worldbooknight.org	**24** Babytime (ages 0-2) 10:00am Native Plant Meeting 7:00pm	**25** Emergent Reader Story Time (ages 4-6) 10:00am	**26**
27	**28**	**29** Emergent Reader Story Time (ages 4-6) 10:00am Neverland Book Club 7:00pm	**30** Toddler Story Time (ages 2-3) 10:00am	**MAC READS** 2014 Join us for the tenth annual MacReads, a community-wide book reading and discussion that culminates in a presentation by the choice author. The 2014 MacReads book is *Shards* by Ismet Prcic. Join us at Linfield's Nicholson Library at 7:30pm on May 1st.		

ala.org
atyourlibrary.org

celebrate
NATIONAL LIBRARY WEEK
April 13-19, 2014

From *Crash Course in Marketing for Libraries: Second Edition* by Susan W. Alman and Sara Gillespie Swanson. Santa Barbara, CA: Libraries Unlimited. Copyright © 2015.

May 2014

READ·LEARN·GROW·INQUIRE
McMINNVILLE·PUBLIC
L I B R A R Y
225 NW Adams Street : (503) 435 - 5562
McMinnville, OR 97128 : www.maclibrary.org

Sunday 1pm-5pm	Monday Closed	Tuesday 10am-8pm	Wednesday 10am-8pm	Thursday 10am-8pm	Friday 10am-5pm	Saturday 1pm-5pm
	Join us for the tenth annual MacReads, a community-wide book reading and discussion that culminates in a presentation by the choice author. The 2014 MacReads book is *Shards* by Ismet Prcic. Schools, book clubs and residents throughout Yamhill County are encouraged to participate. Join us at Linfield's Nicholson Library at 7:30pm on May 1st.			**1** Babytime 10:00am MacReads: Ismet Prcic will discuss Shards at Linfield Library at 7:30pm	**2** Emergent Reader Story Time (ages 4-6) 10:00am	**3**
4	**5** Cat Coalition Meeting 10:00am Yamhill County Slow Food Meeting 6:00pm	**6** Emergent Reader Story Time (ages 4-6) 10:00am	**7** Toddler Story Time (ages 2-3) 10:00am First Wednesday Book Club 2:00pm Teen Council 4:15pm	**8** Babytime (ages 0-2) 10:00am Friends Meeting noon	**9** Emergent Reader Story Time (ages 4-6) 10:00am	**10** Book Sale 10:00am-2:00pm Doors open at 9:00am for current Friends of the Library members
11	**12** La Leche Meeting 9:00am Mac ATC Make and Trade Group 6:00pm	**13** Emergent Reader Story Time (ages 4-6) 10:00am Book Group 7:00pm	**14** Toddler Story Time (ages 2-3) 10:00am	**15** Babytime (ages 0-2) 10:00am	**16** Emergent Reader Story Time (ages 4-6) 10:00am	**17**
18	**19**	**20**	**21** Kiddo's Play Time 10:00am	**22** Native Plant Meeting 7:00pm	**23**	**24**
25	**26** Together Works LGBT support group 6:00pm	**27** Neverland Book Club 7:00pm	**28** Kiddo's Play Time 10:00am	**29**	**30**	**31**

[MAC READS 2014]

SHARDS
ISMET PRCIC

McMinnville Public
Library Book Discussion
Tuesday, April 8 at 7:00pm
McMinnville Public Library's
Carnegie Room

Author Talk
with Ismet Prcic
Thursday, May 1 at 7:30pm
Nicholson Library
Linfield College

McMinnville Public Library

Treasurer's Report
By Loretta Hawley

In the period October 2013 through December 2013, the Friends had income of $4,289.88 and expenses of $1,037.03.

Income:		
$ 336.00	from memorial/celebration fund
1,940.00	from memberships
1,168.50	from book sales
485.38	from lobby book sales
360.00	from donations
4,289.88	Total

Expenditures:	
60.00	Newsletter expense
258.50	Friends gifts to the library
330.00	Children's program
25.49	Misc.
15.04	Adult program
348.00	Book Bags
1,037.03	Total

Dear Friends,

Our January book sale was a huge success, but we still have a large quantity books, CDs, and DVDs available for our March 15th and May 10th sales and more keep rolling in. We need volunteers to help with the set up of the sales (Friday, March 14th and May 9th). We also need help on the dates of the book sales. Volunteers who work the set ups get first pick of possible treasures. We're constantly looking for new helpers (1:00 - 3:00pm on the Fridays before the sales and 9:00 am-3:00 pm on Saturdays). You can reserve your preferences by calling Ken Carter (916-524-8147) or by emailing me at eoghnri@hotmail.com. All inquiries will be answered.

Thanks,
Ken Carter, Book Sale Coordinator

Benefactors

Jennifer Berg
Gary and Diane Buckley
Robert and Carol Dodge
Matt and Katie Gerbrandt
Lee and Barbara Howard
Neil and Judith Kunze
Gloria Lutz
Julia Meck
Mary Martin
Berniece Owen
Vaughan Palmore
Ilsa Perse
Steven Rupp
Neil and Gerry Steller
Joyce and Bob Wolcott

Donors

Pamela Bergen
Marilyn Boyd (Berg)
Norma Kidwell Brott
Gus and Cathy Carstensen
Kim Ednie and Rommel Raj
Mike and Gretchen Freeman
Don and Linda Gilbert
Ruth Juda
Martha A. Karson
Vincent Lowe
Ruth and Richard Miller
Norma E Nellis
Jacqueline and Gerald Painter
Denise Patton
Jay and Becky Pearson
George and Karen Ray
Patty and Rick Sorensen
Dee Staple
Mark and Jennifer Trumbo

Supporters

Laurel and Janet Adams
Barbara and Bruce Anderson
Mary Bates Anderson
Amy and Jason Bizon
Mary Chase Bublitz
Doug and Linda Cruikshank
Charlyn Dalebout
Beth Dell
Jennie Sue Dunn-Dixon and Joe Dixon
Linda Foley
June Foster
Zachary and Samantha Geary
Dan Hilbert
Margaret Lee
Trudy Mackel
Tim and Diane Marsh
Ken and Jane Myers
Robert Myers
Patti Pavelich
Lynda Phillippi
Jacqueline Salkield
Liz and Mike Santone
Joyce Siegel
Phyllis Stearns
Frankie L. Williams

Newsletter design and editing by
Kirsten Stoller & Julia Meck

FRIENDS OF McMINNVILLE LIBRARY
225 NW Adams Street
McMinnville, OR 97128

READ·LEARN·GROW·INQUIRE
McMINNVILLE·PUBLIC
L I B R A R Y

YOU ARE INVITED TO JOIN

The Friends of McMinnville Public Library

We support the community by:
• Purchasing new books • Fundraising with used book sales • Sponsoring programs and
author talks • Volunteering in all areas of the library • Providing funds for small projects •
Promoting Memorial and Celebration Books

Name:

Address:

Phone:

Please provide your e-mail if you would like to go "paperless." The
newsletter is published in March, June, September, and
December. If you provide your e-mail we will e-mail a digital copy
to you rather than mail a paper copy.

E-mail address

Please check your membership level. Mail check & completed form to:
Friends of McMinnville Library
225 NW Adams St
McMinnville, OR 97128

Membership Levels & Rates	
☐ Single	$10 per year
☐ Family	$15 per year
☐ Supporter	$35-$74 per year
☐ Donor	$75-$149 per year
☐ Benefactor	$150-plus per year
☐ Business Membership	$250 per year

Thank You

Appendix K

Sample Press Release

Awards

The Lackawanna County Commissioners issued a proclamation declaring September 12, 2006, "Abington Community Library Day." The proclamation came in response to the Library's recognition as one of three libraries to receive the annual Marketing Award from the Office of Commonwealth Libraries in June 2006. In 2007 the Library recognized new IDEAL PATRONs: First Lady Laura Bush, and the Honorable Tom Ridge and his wife Michele. The Library has consistently been voted #1 in the Best of the Abingtons as "Child-Centered Activity" with staff winning as librarians.

Most recently: Library Recognized for Award

By Leah Rudolph

The Abington Community Library in Clarks Summit received the annual Pennsylvania Library Association (PaLA) Library Support Staff Recognition Award. This award is presented to a library that has consistently encouraged and supported participation in career development activities, particularly those of PaLA, by support staff in Pennsylvania libraries. The award is presented to a library, not to a staff member.

It goes to a library that consistently:

- provides staff with opportunities to develop library skills through continuing education opportunities;

- allows staff to attend PaLA conferences and Chapter Meetings as a Support Staff member;

- provides staff with opportunities to take classes on library related activities or in areas that they can use on the job.

Staff member Sandy Longo nominated the Abington Community Library based on the strong support of the library director and trustees, who have recognized that a well-trained and highly motivated staff is essential. Staff has taken part in workshops and continuing education programs

199

organized by the Lackawanna County Library System and relevant webinars, events organized by the Northeast Chapter of the PaLA, PaLA Annual Conference, and PaLA's Academy for Leadership Studies. In addition, staff has been encouraged to pursue degrees in Library Science, creating an educated and qualified leadership pool from which to draw upon in the future. The award was presented to the library at the PaLA Annual Conference in November, and then presented to the Board of Trustees by PaLA Northeast Chapter Chair Sheli McHugh.

If you aren't making mistakes, then you aren't trying enough new things.

*Follow us on Twitter (**abingtoncomlib**) and 'like' **Abington Community Library** on Facebook! You'll be glad you did as we are committed to lifelong learning.*

Index

About the Authors

SUSAN W. ALMAN is a lecturer at San Jose State University, San Jose, California, and she has held teaching posts at the University of Michigan and University of Pittsburgh. She has experience in marketing and public relations for public, academic, and special libraries as a teacher and practitioner. Her published works include ABC-CLIO's *Designing Online Learning: A Primer for Librarians*. Alman holds a PhD degree in library science from the University of Pittsburgh.

SARA GILLESPIE SWANSON is the assistant director for information literacy at Davidson College, Davidson, North Carolina. She holds a master's in English from the University of Chicago and a master's in library and information science from the University of Pittsburgh.